Vanilla

Vanilla

Cooking with one of the world's finest ingredients

Janet Sawyer

photography by Steve Painter

LONDON · NEW YORK

To all Little Podders everywhere,
especially Chris White,
who has extremely good taste!

DESIGN, PHOTOGRAPHY AND PROP STYLING Steve Painter
COMMISSIONING EDITOR Nathan Joyce
HEAD OF PRODUCTION Patricia Harrington
ART DIRECTOR Leslie Harrington
EDITORIAL DIRECTOR Julia Charles
PUBLISHER Cindy Richards

FOOD STYLIST Lucy McKelvie
INDEXER Diana Le Core

First published in 2014 by
Ryland Peters & Small
20–21 Jockey's Fields
London WC1R 4BW
and
519 Broadway, 5th Floor
New York, NY 10012

www.rylandpeters.com

10 9 8 7 6 5 4 3 2 1
Text © Janet Sawyer 2014
Design and photographs © Ryland Peters & Small 2014 except p65 © Will Halfacree

Printed in China

ISBN: 978-1-84975-566-5

A CIP record for this book is available from the British Library.
US Library of Congress CIP data has been applied for.

NOTES
• All spoon measurements are level unless otherwise specified.
• All eggs are medium (UK) or large (US), unless otherwise specified. Uncooked or partially cooked eggs should not be served to the very old, frail, young children, pregnant women or those with compromised immune systems.
• When a recipe calls for the grated zest of citrus fruit, buy unwaxed fruit and wash well before using. If you can only find treated fruit, scrub well in warm soapy water before using.
• Ovens should be preheated to the specified temperatures. We recommend using an oven thermometer. If using a fan-assisted oven, adjust temperatures according to the manufacturer's instructions.

contents

Introduction

'Ah, you flavour everything; you are the vanilla of society' **Sydney Smith (1771–1845), English writer**

The above quote from a father to his daughter in 1845 was intended as a great compliment. He certainly was not referring to her as a 'plain Jane'. It is extraordinary that the perception of vanilla has changed so dramatically that were Lord Sidney Smith to say the same today he would most probably be given a good slap by his daughter.

Once treasured as 'black gold' (for its rarity was more precious than gold), it is time for vanilla to regain its original status and value. During the course of this book, I hope that you will become more informed and passionate about this remarkable orchid (and the wonderful fruit that it yields) and the soil and toil behind its cultivation.

The aroma of vanilla is so familiar to us all. It is present in many of the products we purchase, from perfumes and cosmetics to the dishes that we order in restaurants around the world. Yet for years, you may have been deprived of its full benefits, unwittingly purchasing imitation vanilla. However, those in the know will always have real vanilla in their store cupboards or pantries.

This book will alert you to the reasons why we should be choosing real vanilla, encourage you to become enthusiastic about its magical qualities and hopefully convince you to become an advocate for its revival in the kitchen. I sincerely hope that you will demand real vanilla when you are purchasing your next ice cream!

How To Use Vanilla

'There are two spiritual dangers in not owning a farm. One is the danger of supposing that breakfast comes from the grocery, and the other that heat comes from the furnace.' **Aldo Leopold (1887–1948), American author and scientist**

Vanilla, as well as being used as a flavour in its own right, has four basic attributes. It:
- tempers bitterness (for example, removing unwanted bitterness of chocolate)
- adds to fruitiness
- enhances sweetness (and in fact can act as a substitute for a certain amount of sugar in your cooking)
- is a perfect flavour-partner for a wide range of herbs, fruits and spices, including: thyme, juniper, chilli/chile, chocolate, basil, cardamom, coriander/cilantro, dates, fennel, ginger, mint and tarragon.

There are a variety of vanilla products that can be utilized in the kitchen. The most commonly used one is vanilla extract, which is made by breaking the vanilla pods/beans into pieces before filtering through alcohol and water. This brings out the all-important vanillin aromas. It is possible to make one's own extract, but it is time-consuming and expensive. If you're a busy person, it's better to purchase a bottle! The shelf life of vanilla extract is around three years, and you can keep it in the store cupboard. Get it out and use it in as much of your cooking as possible! Don't worry about the alcohol content; this simply acts as a carrier to protect the vanilla. It may say 35% alcohol content on the bottle, but it all evaporates once cooked, leaving the essential product intact.

Then, of course, there are the wonderful vanilla pods/beans themselves. To split a pod/bean and remove the seeds, first lay the pod/bean flat on a chopping board. Use a sharp knife to make a vertical cut in the pod/bean and then lay it flat on the surface. Using the back of the knife, put some pressure on the pod/bean and slowly scrape out the seeds in one movement on each half of the pod. Alternatively, butterfly the pod/bean by making a horizontal cut right through the centre of the pod/bean and scrape the seeds out as in the first method. Vanilla pods/beans are much more commonly used in cooking these days. Having said that, until a few years ago, most people would have been suspicious if they saw black seeds in their food; thankfully nowadays, we are more like our European friends, and we demand to see the seeds in our vanilla ice cream. I'm told that a busy restaurant kitchen can get through up to 300 pods/beans a day.

Most people do not realise that you can re-use a vanilla pod/bean (as long as it has not been split). If you wash and dry it after use, you can re-use it two or three times before finally popping it into your sugar jar to let it infuse into vanilla sugar. You can even put the spent pod/bean in a blender and grind it down to make vanilla powder. This can be used to decorate your creams and add a subtle flavour to your desserts.

Vanilla paste is also available (now appearing in a handy tube, which LittlePod introduced to the market several years ago). The content of a tube of vanilla paste is roughly equivalent to 20 vanilla pods/beans, but the paste is so versatile and intense that only a small amount is required. It is an easy way to use vanilla, and I can't recommend it highly enough. Tom Beeston, of Eat England, calls LittlePod's vanilla paste a 'much-needed evolution in the kitchen.' Very importantly, our paste formulation also ensures that very little vanilla flavour is baked off during cooking.

There are some more creative uses for vanilla as well:

• add a pod/bean to your oils (groundnut, olive, etc.) to give an extra dimension to cooking or to salad dressings

• add to cocktails, like mojitos and piña coladas, or just rub some vanilla round the top of the glass when making margaritas

• make a vanilla tea by roughly grinding a dried vanilla pod/bean and tumbling it into your favourite blend, such as Assam

• vanilla is also a well-known deodorizer, so adding a few drops to an oil burner will absorb cooking smells and keep the kitchen smelling fragrant

Cookies
& Small Cakes

Very Vanilla Shortbread

This recipe is the creation of Little Pod's development chef Dave Buchanan. Having been daring enough to tamper with the holy porridge when we launched in Scotland, we continued being very Scottish for the whole occasion, and Dave was all kilted up while demonstrating how he makes his granny's shortbread, which he suffused with our vanilla paste. It became such a winner that it's still a regular taster bake for every event we attend – people love it. You must, however, be very careful when adding the vanilla. Too soon and the mixture will coagulate; too late and it will not combine properly. You'll know the right moment: just before the dough comes together. Have a go! We haven't got as far as vanilla haggis yet, but you never know, come Burns night...

**225 g/1¾ cups plain/
all-purpose flour**

100 g/¾ cup semolina

225 g/2 sticks butter

**100 g/½ cup caster/granulated
sugar**

**1 tablespoon LittlePod vanilla
paste, or 3 vanilla pods/beans,
(seeds only, see pages 8–9)**

**25 g/2 tablespoons
demerara/turbinado sugar, for
dusting**

**a 30 x 22.5-cm/12 x 9-inch
baking pan, greased**

makes 12–14 fingers

Mix the flour and semolina together in a bowl, add the butter and sugar and mix it with your hands until it starts to come together. It is crucial that you add the vanilla paste or seeds at this point, before the mixture completely binds together, so that it disperses evenly. Knead with your hands until a dough forms.

Press the dough into the prepared baking pan, spreading it out evenly with a knife or spatula. Use a fork to prick it all over. Place in the fridge to cool until firm. Meanwhile, preheat the oven to 160°C (325°F) Gas 3.

Remove the shortbread from the fridge and bake for about 35 minutes, or until it is a pale golden-brown colour. Sprinkle the demerara/turbinado sugar over the top, then leave to cool for 5 minutes. Cut it up however you like (we like to cut ours into bite-sized squares or fingers) and place on a wire rack to finish cooling before tucking in.

Cardamom & Vanilla Cookies

We met Indian chef Manju Malhi early on in the LittlePod story. Manju loved the smell and aroma associated with vanilla, but she did not use it in her cooking at that time. All that has since changed! Whenever she's in India she is constantly asked to prepare tea parties, complete with desserts, and when she's in the UK she has found that vanilla enlivens the spices in her dishes. As a LittlePod friend we make sure her cupboard is always well stocked. The vanilla rounds out the spice in this perfect crisp snack to serve with tea, mango juice or even Vanilla Lassi (see page 108). Cut them to the size of petits fours.

50 g/¼ cup caster/granulated sugar

50 g/3 tablespoons butter

2 teaspoons LittlePod vanilla paste, or 2 vanilla pods/beans, (seeds only, see pages 8–9)

4 green cardamom pods, seeds only, crushed

75 g/⅔ cup plain/all-purpose flour, sifted

75 g/⅔ cup wholemeal/whole-wheat flour

50 g/⅓ cup fine semolina

makes 16–18

Preheat the oven to 190°C (375°F) Gas 5 and grease a baking sheet.

In a bowl, cream together the sugar and butter with a wooden spoon until light and fluffy. Beat in the vanilla paste and cardamom; then add the flours and semolina. Mix to a firm paste and gently knead it for 5 minutes. The dough will be quite crumbly.

Dust your hands with flour. Use your fingers to form golf-ball-sized pieces of dough and flatten them into circles about 1.5 cm/¾ inch thick, or roll out the dough and cut out circles with a 7.5-cm/3-inch cookie cutter.

Place them on the baking sheet, at least 2.5 cm/1 inch apart, and bake for 12–15 minutes, or until light brown. Cool on a wire rack.

Store in an airtight container for up to 3 weeks – if they don't get gobbled up before then!

Peanut Butter Cookies

This recipe comes from Little Pod's designer, Harriet. We can't help peeking at her diet blog from time to time. Who would have thought that vanilla would round out the taste of peanut butter?

125 g/1 cup spelt flour (or wholemeal/whole-wheat flour)

1 teaspoon baking powder

1 teaspoon salt

225 g/1 cup peanut butter (preferably smooth, or you can use crunchy)

170 g/¾ cup agave syrup (available in larger supermarkets/grocery stores; replace with maple syrup if you can't find it)

75 ml/⅓ cup olive oil

1 teaspoon vanilla extract

40 g/¼ cup cacao nibs (sold in wholefood shops/stores; if you can't find them, use roughly grated very dark/bittersweet chocolate)

makes 10–12

Preheat the oven to 180°C (350°F) Gas 4 and line a baking sheet with baking paper. Place the oven shelves in the top third of the oven.

In a mixing bowl, combine the flour, baking powder and salt. Put the peanut butter, agave syrup, olive oil, vanilla extract and cacao nibs in a separate, larger bowl, and stir until combined.

Pour the flour mixture over the peanut butter mixture and stir until barely combined; it will still be a bit 'dusty' looking. Set aside for 5 minutes, then give it one more quick stir.

Now drop tablespoons of the batter onto the prepared baking sheet and press down gently on each one with the back of a fork. It's a loose batter, so if you're set on making criss-cross patterns, it's often easier to chill the batter for an hour or so beforehand.

Bake for 10–11 minutes, but be careful not to overcook, or they may dry out. Leave to cool for 5 minutes, then transfer to a wire cooling rack.

Butternut Squash Cupcakes with Orange Icing

Butternut squash is one of those 'power' foods, and is such a gift in the autumnal garden. This year, a plant of ours produced 12 squash. If you want to tempt your children with a vegetable cake, this is the one. The recipe was devised by two young mums, Jacqui and Emma, who contacted me one Christmas to buy products for their hampers. They can now be found running their own successful deli-café, Hills & Parkes, in Honor Oak, south London. Well done to them!

130 g/4½ oz. butternut squash

225 g/2 sticks butter, at room temperature

240 g/1¼ cups soft light brown sugar

2 UK large/US extra large eggs

½ teaspoon vanilla extract

120 g/1 cup self-raising/self-rising flour

120 g/1 cup plain/all-purpose flour

½ teaspoon ground ginger

1½ teaspoons mixed spice

125 ml/½ cup sour cream

175 g/6 oz. cream cheese, at room temperature

½ teaspoon LittlePod vanilla paste or ½ a vanilla pod/bean, (seeds only, see pages 8–9)

450 g/3 cups icing/confectioners' sugar, sifted, plus extra for dusting

grated zest of 2 oranges

physalis/Cape gooseberries, to serve

a 12-hole muffin pan lined with tall cupcake cases/liners

makes 12

Preheat the oven to 180°C (350°F) Gas 4. Peel, then steam the squash over a pan of boiling water for 30 minutes. Once soft, put it in a shallow bowl and mash it to a soft pulp with a fork. Pass it through a sieve/strainer to remove any lumps and make a lovely, rich purée. Let it stand to get rid of any excess water.

Cream 110 g/7 tablespoons of the butter with the sugar until pale and smooth, then add the eggs one at a time. Add the vanilla extract, then fold in the puréed squash. Sift the flours, ginger and ½ teaspoon of the mixed spice into a bowl. Slowly add the flour mixture to the butter mixture, then add the sour cream until combined. Carefully spoon the mixture to fill the cupcake cases/liners approximately two-thirds full. Bake for 25 minutes, or until golden brown. Check that the cakes are done by inserting a skewer into the centre of one of them – it should come out clean. Remove from the oven and set aside to cool completely.

To make the cream cheese icing/frosting, soften the remaining butter, add the cream cheese and beat together thoroughly. Add the vanilla paste or seeds. Add the icing/confectioners' sugar and stir to make a smooth, delicious cream; then slowly fold through 1 teaspoon mixed spice and the orange zest. Decorate the cakes with the icing/frosting, using a palette knife/icing spatula or piping/pastry bag, and top with an opened physalis/Cape gooseberry and a light dusting of icing/confectioners' sugar.

LittlePod Scones

There is nothing more Devon than a cream tea. These scones are best served slightly warm, either with a little butter or with clotted cream and strawberry jam. However, the layering of the cream and jam is a contentious issue. In Devon, it is customary to put the jam on first and the cream on top, but in neighbouring Cornwall it is customary to put the cream on first and the jam on top. Which side are you on?

a few drops of lemon juice

150 ml/⅔ cup milk

225 g/1¾ cups plain/all-purpose flour, plus extra for dusting

4 teaspoons baking powder

½ teaspoon salt

30 g/2 tablespoons butter

1 teaspoon vanilla extract

milk or flour to glaze

makes 12

Preheat the oven to 230°C (450°F) Gas 8. Stir the lemon juice into the milk and leave it to stand for 10 minutes. Sift the flour, baking powder and salt into a bowl. Cut the butter into the flour and rub it in until the mixture resembles fine breadcrumbs. Stir the vanilla extract into the milk and make a well in the centre of the flour mixture. Pour the milk mixture into the well, then quickly stir it in until a light, springy dough forms (you may need to add a few drops of water to keep it light).

Sprinkle a baking sheet with flour and place it in the oven to heat up. Flour a work surface lightly, then turn out the dough onto it and knead it lightly. Roll it out until it is around 1.5 cm/¾ inch thick and cut out rounds with a 6-cm/2½-inch cookie cutter. Brush the scones with milk for a glazed finish, or flour for a soft finish. Place on the preheated baking sheet and bake for 10–12 minutes, or until golden brown.

Vanilla & Amaretto Macaroons

Macaroons are an Italian favourite; they are eaten as petit fours with coffee, or broken into pieces and added to desserts or ice cream. This recipe is also gluten-free. The vanilla paste works especially well with gluten-free flour, and helps it rise.

2 sheets rice paper

100 g/⅔ cup ground almonds/almond meal

2 tablespoons gluten-free or rice flour

220 g/1 cup plus 2 tablespoons caster/granulated sugar

1½ teaspoons Amaretto liqueur

½ teaspoon LitlePod vanilla paste or ½ a vanilla pod/bean, (seeds only, see pages 8–9)

3 egg whites

12 blanched almonds, split

makes 24

Preheat the oven to 180°C (350°F) Gas 4 and line a baking sheet with rice paper. Mix the ground almonds/almond meal, flour and sugar together in a bowl. Combine the Amaretto and vanilla paste or seeds with 2 of the egg whites, then stir them into the flour mixture.

Transfer the mixture to a food processor and process to a smooth paste, then place it in a piping/pastry bag fitted with a 1.5-cm/¾-inch nozzle/tip. Pipe 2.5-cm/1-inch diameter rounds onto the rice paper. Flatten each one slightly .

Beat the remaining egg white. Place a split blanched almond on top of each macaroon, then brush it with the beaten egg white. Bake for 20 minutes, or until nicely browned.

Cool on a wire rack, then cut out the rice paper around each of the macaroons.

Chocolate Éclairs with Crème Pâtissière

One evening we were invited to a 'bring & share' supper at Darts Farm, our local farm shop. The evening was to welcome students from the University of Gastronomic Sciences in Italy, and was hosted by the local Slow Food movement. We decided to make a very long chocolate éclair rather than making profiteroles, and we shaped it into the LittlePod flower motif. We placed it in the centre of the display table and, when we returned for pudding, it was all gone – the students had beaten us to it!

FOR THE CHOUX PASTRY:

40 g/3 scant tablespoons butter

75 g/⅔ cup plain/all-purpose flour, sifted

2 eggs, lightly beaten

FOR THE CRÈME PÂTISSIÈRE:

3 egg yolks

60 g/⅓ cup caster/granulated sugar

20 g/2½ tablespoons plain/all-purpose flour

1 vanilla pod/bean, split

250 ml/1 cup milk

FOR THE CHOCOLATE TOPPING:

120 g/4 oz. dark/bittersweet chocolate

120 ml/½ cup double/heavy cream

1 teaspoon Cointreau or rum

makes 12

First, make the choux pastry. Preheat the oven to 220°C (425°F) Gas 7 and line a baking sheet with baking paper. Melt the butter with 50 ml/3 tablespoons plus 1 teaspoon water in a pan over medium heat, making sure none evaporates. Once melted, bring to the boil and remove from the heat. Immediately pour in the flour and beat with a spoon until smooth. Return to the heat and beat until a ball forms, leaving the sides of the pan clean. Let the mixture cool a little, then slowly add the eggs, beating thoroughly between each addition.

Place the choux paste in a piping/pastry bag with a 1-cm/½-inch nozzle/tip and pipe 6–8-cm/2½–3¼-inch lengths on the baking tray/sheet. Bake for 20 minutes, or until firm and dark golden.

For the crème pâtissière, put the egg yolks and 25 g/1½ tablespoons sugar in a bowl and whisk until pale. Add the flour and whisk again. Put the split vanilla pod/bean, remaining sugar and milk in a pan and simmer for 5 minutes. Remove the vanilla pod/bean, pour some of the hot milk over the egg mixture, then return this to the pan with the rest of the milk. Slowly bring to the boil and cook for 2 more minutes. Transfer to another dish to cool, covered with clingfilm/plastic wrap or icing/confectioners' sugar to prevent a skin forming.

For the chocolate topping, break the chocolate into small pieces in a heatproof bowl. Bring the cream to boiling point over a medium heat, then pour the hot cream over the chocolate and stir until it melts and is smooth. Stir in the Cointreau or rum. Set aside for 10 minutes.

To assemble, split the éclairs, fill with crème pâtissière and spread the chocolate topping on top.

Coffee Éclairs with Almond Filling

Unusual things often seem to happen to me, and this was one of the most thrilling. On being awarded my British Empire Medal, I received an invitation to the royal garden party at Buckingham Palace. It was such a joy to walk through the state rooms, out onto the terrace and into the gardens. There were bands playing, cups of barley water to drink, and, of course, the wonderful tea itself, with wonderful éclairs. I made a promise to myself that I would always make éclairs for my garden parties in honour of that memorable day.

FOR THE CHOUX PASTRY:

75 g/⅔ cup plain/all-purpose flour, sifted

40 g/scant 3 tablespoons butter

2 eggs, beaten

FOR THE ALMOND FILLING:

160 g/1 generous cup blanched almonds

2 teaspoons clear honey

¼ teaspoon LittlePod vanilla paste or ¼ of a vanilla pod/bean, (seeds only, see pages 8–9)

FOR THE COFFEE TOPPING:

125 g/½ cup plus 1 tablespoon soft dark brown sugar

2 tablespoons double/heavy cream

60 g/4 tablespoons butter

20 ml/4 teaspoons espresso-strength coffee

1 teaspoon LittlePod coffee extract or 2 tablespoons very strong black coffee

175 g/1¼ cups icing/confectioners' sugar

makes 12

First, make the choux pastry. Preheat the oven to 220°C (425°F) Gas 7 and line a baking sheet with baking paper. Melt the butter with 50 ml/3 tablespoons plus 1 teaspoon water in a pan over medium heat, making sure none evaporates. Once melted, bring to the boil and remove from the heat. Immediately pour in the flour and beat with a spoon until smooth. Return to the heat and beat until a ball forms, leaving the sides of the pan clean. Let the mixture cool a little, then slowly add the eggs, beating thoroughly between each addition.

Place the choux paste in a piping/pastry bag with a 1-cm/½-inch nozzle/tip and pipe 6–8-cm/2½–3¼-inch lengths on the baking sheet. Bake for 20 minutes, or until firm and dark golden.

For the almond filling, process the almonds in a blender with the honey and vanilla paste or seeds. Still blending, slowly add enough water to make a soft, thick paste.

For the coffee topping, place all the ingredients except the icing/confectioners' sugar in a pan and cook over medium heat until the sugar has dissolved. Take off the heat and whisk in the icing/confectioners' sugar. Allow to cool before coating the éclairs.

To assemble, split the éclairs and fill them with almond paste. Spread some coffee topping on each éclair.

The History of Vanilla

The Totonac people of Mexico, a peaceable and artistic community, have always respected their native vanilla plant, which they call *xanath*. The fruit of the *xanath* was imbued with spiritual connotations, and was considered, in accordance with the origin of the word, a 'gift from the Gods'. Vanilla continues to have a sacred place in the lives of the Totonacs today.

Founded in the 1200s, the Totonac city of Papantla was central to a sophisticated trade route through Mesoamerica. During the Aztec empire, vanilla was stored as a rarity and was jealously sought after; its value transcended money. Eventually the paradise of the Totonacs was torn apart by the warring Aztecs, who became intoxicated with the scent of the vanilla orchid and taxed the Totonacs for part of their yearly crop. In fact, only Aztec royalty used vanilla. Having only seen the black seeds of the fruit, they mistakenly called it *tlilxochitl* ('black flower'), and considered it more rare and precious than gold.

Hernán Cortés, one of the Spanish conquerers, arrived in Mexico in 1600, and the Totonacs helped him explore the area. Cortés was awe-struck by the beauty of Tenochtitlan, which he saw as a sophisticated city of refinement with enchanting floating gardens and wonderful architecture. The Spanish called the newly discovered product *vania*, which means 'sheath' or 'pod' The first written reference to the word 'vanilla' appeared over half a century later in a work by William Piso, published in Amsterdam in 1658.

The Aztecs made an intoxicating combination of vanilla and cocoa called *xocolatl*, the first known perfect partnership of chocolate and vanilla, which seduced Cortés. In 1518, Bernal Díaz, a soldier and historian who accompanied Cortés, described seeing the Aztec emperor Montezuma's servants bringing him 'a drink made from the cocoa plant, in cups of pure gold', which he drank before visiting his wives. It was thought of by the Spanish soldiers as 'the divine drink which builds up resistance and fights fatigue'. Díaz brought this delicious drink back to Europe, where it became the secret pleasure of the aristocracy across the continent.

Such was the desire for vanilla that in 1601, when Hugh Morgan, apothecary to Queen Elizabeth I, declared that vanilla should be used as a flavour in its own right, the Queen demanded that it be used in practically everything she ate.

By the eighteenth century, vanilla was very popular in France, so much so that it became a commodity grown in the French colonies. The Isle de Réunion (also known as the Isle de Bourbon) exhibited the perfect conditions for growing the plant, and it is here that the vanilla industry really began. Vanilla is now grown in Madagascar, the Philippines, Indonesia, India, Tahiti, the West Indies, and also in many countries in mainland Africa.

The Marquis of Blandford (later the fifth Duke of Malborough) imported vanilla to Britain in the late eighteenth century. Unfortunately, he accrued significant debts, and was forced to sell his home and possessions, effectively scattering his botanical collection far and wide. However, the botanist and founder-member of the Royal Horticultural Society, Charles Greville, managed to take a cutting of the vanilla orchid from Blandford's glasshouse. Based on a number of artistic drawings, it is believed that the orchid flowered in the gardens of Greville's Paddington home, creating quite a stir (as it was a remarkable botanical event) and a fascination with taking more cuttings. It is thanks to Greville's interest that cuttings from his plant were sent to the botanical gardens at Liège in Belgium. From there the vine spawned an entire industry.

However, the love of the unique 'hidden orchid' remained, and today the vanilla orchid is a prized plant in the Palm House in Kew Gardens, London, where it is hand-pollinated. It is also brought to flower in one of the biospheres at the Eden Project in Cornwall. Given that the flowers only last a day, it is a real treat for those who are there to witness it.

Vanilla growing and curing in Mexico ceased in the 1950s after the harvests were affected by a great drop in temperatures, and Mexican vanilla has since become a rarity. Today, the rise in culinary expertise and an interest in luxury foods have meant that vanilla is once again being recognized as an essential ingredient for food-lovers around the world.

Large Bakes

Elderflower & Almond Cake

I think it's true to say that there is a cake for everyone. Baking is in vogue at the moment, and home cooks are skilling up and hosting cake-making parties, where they often want to make something special. So it was for LittlePod's Clara, who had cooked for herself at university but by her own admission was not an ambitious baker. Nevertheless, she has rolled up her sleeves and put on her apron many a time to prepare for LittlePod gatherings, and this is one of her favourites.

80 g/⅔ cup self-raising/self-rising flour

1 teaspoon baking powder

170 g/1¼ cups ground almonds/almond meal

225 g/2 sticks softened butter

240 g/1 cup plus 3 tablespoons golden caster sugar/raw cane sugar

finely grated zest of 1 lemon

4 eggs, lightly beaten

160 ml/⅔ cup elderflower cordial (use the sort that needs diluting about 1:10)

freshly squeezed juice of 1 lemon

150 ml/⅔ cup mascarpone

150 ml/⅔ cup double/heavy cream

1 teaspoon LittlePod vanilla paste, or 1 vanilla pod/bean, (seeds only, see pages 8–9)

a handful of chopped pistachios

a 23-cm/9-inch springform cake pan, greased and base lined with baking paper

serves 12

Preheat the oven to 180°C (350°F) Gas 4. Mix together the flour, baking powder and almonds. In a separate bowl, cream the butter, 225 g/1 cup plus 2 tablespoons sugar and lemon zest until fluffy. Gradually beat in the eggs, one at a time, making sure that each one is incorporated before adding the next. Quickly beat in the flour mixture, then spoon into the prepared pan and smooth the top. Bake for 40–45 minutes, or until risen and golden.

While the cake is baking, combine 100 ml/scant ½ cup of the elderflower cordial with the lemon juice and remaining sugar. Remove the cake from the oven, then prick it all over and sprinkle the syrup over the surface, guiding the liquid towards the holes. Leave to cool in the pan, then remove.

Put the mascarpone in a bowl with the remaining elderflower cordial and whisk until smooth. Add the cream and vanilla paste or seeds and whisk again to make a softly spreadable icing/frosting. Spread the icing/frosting over the top of the cooled cake and scatter with the chopped pistachios.

Apple & Blueberry Cake

Every week I visit my friend Judy for my piano lesson. One autumnal day, we ventured out apple-picking in Judy's orchard to collect supplies to make her twist on a Mary Berry favourite. It's easy and quick to make, and you can vary the fruit according to the season. It can be enjoyed as a pudding with LittlePod custard (see page 58), or as an afternoon cake.

300 g/10 oz. apples (preferably Granny Smiths)

100 g/⅔ cup blueberries

1 tablespoon brandy or dark rum

1 vanilla pod/bean

230 g/1¾ cups self-raising/self-rising flour

1 heaped teaspoon baking powder

230 g/1 cup plus 2½ tablespoons caster/granulated sugar

2 eggs

1 teaspoon LittlePod vanilla paste or vanilla extract

150 g/1 stick plus 2 tablespoons butter

a handful of raw flaked/slivered almonds or pistachios

a 20-cm/8-inch cake pan, greased

serves 8–10

Peel and slice the apples and combine them with the blueberries. Pour over the rum and infuse with the vanilla pod/bean (this can be washed and retained for further use). Set aside for half an hour or so. Preheat the oven to 160°C (325°F) Gas 3.

Sift the flour, baking powder and sugar into a bowl. In a separate bowl, whisk the eggs until fluffy and light, then add the vanilla paste or extract and stir them into the flour mixture. Pour just over half of the mixture into the cake pan, then drain the fruit and arrange it on top. Cover with the rest of the mixture, but don't worry too much about spreading it right over the fruit, as it will spread itself out in the oven. Sprinkle over the flaked/slivered almonds or pistachios.

Bake for 90 minutes, or until golden. Leave to cool in the pan, then turn out.

Chocolate & Beetroot Fudge Cake

This is the most yummy and luxurious of cakes. I love beet(root) in all its forms – baked, pickled, raw – and could eat it every day. For Little Pod's first anniversary, we devised a cake for our special day, which was held at the Chelsea Physic Garden. This recipe was the result. Limpet Barron, who runs the Tangerine Dream Café at the garden, altered the ingredients a little, producing the most moist, memorable cake.

250 g/8 oz. dark/bittersweet chocolate, plus 150 g/5 oz. for the topping

3 eggs

250 g/2¼ cups light muscovado sugar

1 teaspoon LittlePod vanilla paste or 1 vanilla pod/bean, (seeds only, see pages 8–9)

7 tablespoons clear honey

2 teaspoons LittlePod chocolate extract, or add another 25 g/1 oz. dark/bittersweet chocolate

30 g/¼ cup self-raising/self-rising flour

30 g/¼ cup plain/all-purpose flour

¼ teaspoon bicarbonate of soda/baking soda

¼ teaspoon salt

50 g/⅓ cup ground almonds/almond meal

300 g/10 oz. raw beet(root), peeled and finely grated

30 ml/2 tablespoons sunflower oil

1 teaspoon LittlePod coffee extract (optional)

1 teaspoon vanilla extract

a 20-cm/8-inch round cake pan, greased

serves 12

Preheat the oven to 160°C (325°F) Gas 3. Cut a wide strip of baking paper and tie it around the outside of the cake pan, to make a collar that rises 10 cm/4 inches above the top.

Place the chocolate in a heatproof bowl set over a pan of barely simmering water and heat gently until melted. Set aside to cool briefly. In a large mixing bowl, whisk the eggs with the sugar, vanilla paste or seeds, 4 tablespoons honey and chocolate extract (or extra chocolate) for 3 minutes, until pale and fluffy. Next, fold in the flours, bicarbonate of soda/baking soda, salt and almonds.

Drain any excess liquid from the grated beetroot/beets, then fold it into the cake mixture with a spatula, followed by the cooled chocolate and sunflower oil, until completely combined. Pour the mixture into the prepared pan and bake on the middle shelf for 90 minutes. If a knife or skewer inserted into the middle comes out clean, the cake is cooked. Remove from the oven and leave to cool on a wire rack.

To make the topping, melt the remaining chocolate in a heatproof bowl set over a pan of barely simmering water, then remove it from the heat, add the coffee extract (if using) and vanilla extract and the remaining honey. Set aside for 15 minutes before topping the cake with it. Decorate the cake however you wish; we think it looks beautiful with colourful fresh flowers.

The LittlePod Torta

In the late 1800s, the Petracca brothers migrated from a small town in Basilicata, southern Italy, at a time of economic misery, earthquakes and general upheaval. The brothers brought this family recipe with them to England, where one of them started a bakery, and it was eventually handed down (with a few twists) to my husband, David. On a recent visit to Marsico Nuovo in Basilicata, a lovely elderly chef produced her own version. Nothing like LittlePod's, of course, but possibly slightly better!

250 g/2 cups plain/all-purpose flour

50 g/⅓ cup icing/confectioners' sugar, plus extra to dust

125 g/1 stick butter, softened

5 eggs

50 ml/3 tablespoons milk, plus a little extra for the pastry

150 g/1 cup ground almonds/almond meal

150 g/1 cup caster/granulated sugar

zest and juice of 1 medium lemon

zest of ½ orange (optional)

1 teaspoon LittlePod vanilla paste, or 1 vanilla pod/bean, (seeds only, see pages 8–9)

1 teaspoon clear honey (optional)

1 tablespoon limoncello or Cointreau

a handful of flaked/slivered almonds

cream, crème fraîche or ice cream, to serve

a 20-cm/8-inch round flan pan, greased

serves 6–8

Preheat the oven to 180°C (350°F) Gas 4. Sift the flour and icing/confectioners' sugar into a bowl or mixer. Add the butter, 1 egg and a splash of milk. Mix together until it comes together in a ball. Wrap in clingfilm/plastic wrap and place in the fridge for 30 minutes.

Meanwhile, separate the remaining eggs. Sift the almonds and caster/granulated sugar into a bowl. Add the lemon and orange zests (if using), vanilla paste or seeds, honey (if using), lemon juice, milk, limencello or Cointreau and 4 egg yolks. Mix all the ingredients together to make a smooth paste.

Roll out the pastry on a lightly floured surface and use it to line the prepared flan pan. Cover with foil or baking paper and blind bake for 15 minutes, or until golden.

Meanwhile, whisk the egg whites to stiff peaks, then gently fold them into the almond mixture. (Note: for a lighter or a heavier bake, you can add more or less egg white, as you prefer.)

Once the pastry is cooked, fill the pan with the almond mixture and dot with the flaked/slivered almonds. Bake for 25 minutes, or until the top has gently browned. If a knife or skewer inserted into the middle comes out clean, the cake is cooked.

Dust with sifted icing/confectioners' sugar and serve with cream, crème fraîche or ice cream.

Lumberjack Cake

Little Pod supplies the Exploding Bakery, whose pastries travel to London and Paris every day. Its owner, Tom, told me about the origin of one of his favourite cakes: 'Flicking through a copy of Australian Women's Weekly, as I am prone to do, I came across a rather rugged and handsome-looking cake that appealed to all my manly confectionery needs. When it came out of the oven we duly scoffed it down, noting the uncanny resemblance to a sticky toffee pudding: delicious sweet dates and dense, moist sponge. Add to this the apple and crunchy caramelized coconut and you have yourself one hell of a tasty traybake...'

FOR THE CAKE:

250 g/1⅔ cups chopped dried dates

1 teaspoon bicarbonate of soda/baking soda

175 g/1½ sticks butter

300 g/1½ cups caster/granulated sugar

2 eggs

2 teaspoons vanilla extract

400 g/2⅓ cups plain/all-purpose flour

1 teaspoon salt

500 g/1 lb. 2 oz. apples

FOR THE TOPPING:

75 g/5 tablespoons butter

125 g/generous ½ cup soft light brown sugar

100 ml/6 tablespoons milk

70 g/¾ cup desiccated/shredded coconut

a 30 x 18-cm/12 x 7-inch traybake pan, lined with baking paper

serves 8

Preheat the oven to 180°C (350°F) Gas 4. Put the dates in a bowl with the bicarbonate of soda/baking soda, add 330 ml/1⅓ cups boiling water and set aside to cool.

Cream the butter and sugar in a mixing bowl, then add the eggs and vanilla extract. Beat vigorously until fluffy, then gently fold in the flour and salt, taking care not to overmix it.

Peel and remove the cores from the apples, then finely chop them. Stir the apples into the bowl of dates (this will help them cool down). Fold the apples and dates into the cake batter.

Pour into the prepared pan and bake for 40–50 minutes. If a knife or skewer inserted into the middle comes out clean, the cake is cooked.

Meanwhile, make the topping. Place all the ingredients in a heavy-based pan and cook gently over low heat until the butter melts, or heat in a microwave-proof container. Give it a good stir.

Remove the cake from the oven, spoon the topping mixture onto it and spread it out evenly, then return it to the oven for a further 20 minutes, or until the top is golden brown.

Beery Bake Cake

Little Pod goes liquid! When we launched our award-winning vanilla beer we never expected it to end up in a cake. However, some time later I'd had an idea that took me back to my Irish roots, and the result was this — a souped-up version of an Irish porter cake. People often want to make a cake for Christmas but then leave it until it's too late. This quick-to-make cake is the answer. As the Irish say: Nollaig shona duit! (Happy Christmas!).

450 g/1 lb. mixed dried fruit

50 g/2 oz. glacé/candied cherries (optional)

grated zest of 1 orange

1 tablespoon LittlePod chocolate extract or 350 ml/1½ cups LittlePod vanilla beer or stout

350 g/2¾ cups plain/all-purpose flour

¼ teaspoon mixed spice/apple pie spice

175 g/1½ sticks butter or margarine

275 g/1⅓ cups soft brown sugar

50 g/⅓ cup walnuts or 50 g/⅓ cup blanched almonds, shredded

grated zest of 1 lemon

½ teaspoon bicarbonate of soda/baking soda

150 ml/⅔ cup LittlePod vanilla beer or stout

3 eggs

1 teaspoon LittlePod vanilla paste, or 1 vanilla pod/bean, (seeds only, see pages 8–9)

a 20-cm/8-inch round cake pan, greased and lined with baking paper, with a 5-cm/2-inch collar

serves 12

Soak the dried fruit, cherries and orange zest in the chocolate extract overnight (you could also add the juice of the orange for extra orangeyness), or for at least 1 hour. Alternatively, soak the dried fruit, cherries and orange zest in 350 ml/1½ cups of LittlePod vanilla beer or regular stout overnight (or for at least 1 hour).

Preheat the oven to 140°C (275°F) Gas 1. Sift the flour and spice into a mixing bowl. Cut the butter or margarine into the flour and rub it in until it resembles breadcrumbs. Add the sugar, soaked fruit (after straining it), nuts and lemon zest and stir well.

Dissolve the bicarbonate of soda/baking soda in the vanilla beer or stout over a low heat. Beat the eggs, add the vanilla paste or seeds and combine them with the beer mixture, off the heat. Stir this into the dry ingredients and mix well.

Pour into the prepared pan and bake for 2 hours, then turn down the oven to 120°C (250°F), or until nicely browned. If a knife or skewer inserted into the middle comes out clean, the cake is cooked.

Allow to cool in the pan before turning it out. Do not cut it the same day, if possible; it is best kept to mature in an airtight container. If you add extra dried fruit and decorate with marzipan and fondant icing, it makes a perfect (and much less time-consuming) Christmas cake.

Riverford Rum, Raisin & Curd Cheesecake

We're very proud to supply some of the UK's best restaurants, and for a very special birthday I chose to take my family to the Riverford Field Kitchen here in Devon. Renowned for its fantastic organic food grown on the doorstep, its ethos chimes perfectly with Little Pod: simple, natural and wholesome. Thanks to Rob Andrew, their head chef, for sharing this delicious cheesecake recipe.

1 dried allspice berry

1 star anise

a 2.5-cm/1-inch cinnamon stick

70 ml/⅓ cup dark rum

100 g/⅔ cup raisins

115 g/1 stick butter

170 g/6 oz. plain digestive biscuits/graham crackers

170 g/6 oz. ginger biscuits/cookies

425 g/2 cups mascarpone

425 g/2 cups curd cheese

1 teaspoon LittlePod vanilla paste, or 1 vanilla pod/bean, (seeds only, see pages 8–9)

juice and zest of 1 medium orange

6 eggs

285 g/1½ cups caster/granulated sugar

cream, ice cream, fresh strawberries or strawberry coulis, to serve

a 25-cm/10-inch round cake pan, greased

serves 8

Grind the whole spices, then gently warm the rum with the spices. Pour the mixture over the raisins and leave to soak for 30 minutes.

Preheat the oven to 140°C (275°F) Gas 1. Melt the butter in a pan, put the digestive biscuits/graham crackers and ginger biscuits/cookies in a food processor and process to fine crumbs. Pour the crumbs into the butter and stir well. Press the mixture into the base of the prepared pan. Bake for 20 minutes, or until set and golden, while you prepare the filling.

Whisk together the mascarpone, curd cheese and vanilla paste or seeds with the orange zest, adding the orange juice as you go, to form a soft, smooth mixture.

Whisk the eggs and sugar until well combined. Combine the egg mixture with the cheese mixture using a balloon whisk or spatula. Add the raisin and spice mixture and gently stir together. Pour onto the baked biscuit base, filling the pan right to the top.

Bake for 45 minutes, or until the cheesecake has set but still has a wobble. Allow to cool before removing it from the pan.

Apricot & Almond Frangipane Tart

This recipe comes from LittlePod friend and executive chef Leonel Gouveia. Leonel designs and makes magnificent wedding cakes, and joined forces with the Chairman of Devon County Council to cut the ribbon at the opening of our new headquarters in October 2013. You can make this recipe your own by using your favourite home-made jam and topping it with your choice of nuts. The sweet pastry is slightly more time-consuming than regular pastry, but it's worth it. It's a foolproof recipe for frangipane, which you can use in all sorts of desserts, with whatever pastry base you wish.

FOR THE PASTRY:

125 g/1 cup plain/all-purpose flour

a small pinch of salt

40 g/scant ¼ cup icing/confectioners' sugar

zest of ½ lemon

60 g/4 tablespoons butter, cut into pieces

2 egg yolks, beaten

FOR THE FRANGIPANE:

200 g/1 stick plus 5 tablespoons butter

200 g/1¼ cups icing/confectioners' sugar

4 eggs

300 g/2 cups ground almonds/almond meal

½ teaspoon LittlePod vanilla paste, or ½ a vanilla pod/bean, (seeds only, see pages 8–9)

2 tablespoons apricot jam, for spreading

a handful of raw almond flakes/slivers, pine nuts or pistachios, for sprinkling

a 20-cm/8-inch round tart pan, or a 12-hole tartlet pan, greased

serves 8

For the pastry, put 1 tablespoon water in a small bowl and chill it until very cold. Put the flour, salt, sugar and lemon zest in a food processor and blend together for a few seconds. Add the butter and blend briefly until a breadcrumb consistency is achieved. Turn the mixture out into a bowl and add the chilled water and one of the egg yolks. Mix, then knead lightly until a dough forms. Wrap in clingfilm/plastic wrap and refrigerate for at least 1 hour.

Meanwhile, make the frangipane by blending the butter, sugar, eggs, ground almonds/almond meal and vanilla paste or seeds in a food processor or blender until the mixture resembles breadcrumbs.

Preheat the oven to 200°C (400°F) Gas 6.

Take the pastry out of the fridge. Roll it out thinly on a lightly floured surface and use it to line the prepared pan. Return it to the fridge for 30 minutes. Line the pan with baking paper, fill with baking beans/pie weights and bake for 15–20 minutes. Remove the baking paper and baking beans/pie weights, brush with the remaining beaten egg yolk and return to the oven for 5 minutes. Turn the oven down to 180°C (350°F) Gas 4.

Using the back of a teaspoon, spread the jam evenly over the base of the pastry, then fill it with the frangipane mixture. Sprinkle the nuts on top. Bake for 20 minutes, or until lightly golden on top.

Vanilla & Apple Strudel

I was invited by Darts Farm, my local farm shop and demo lab, to take part in a local food show in their very own teepee with a wood-fired oven. I wanted the demo to be interactive and thought strudel would be very good because people could make their own parcels, which would cook quickly in front of them. The smell of the vanilla drew the crowds in!

FOR THE PASTRY:

100 g/¾ cup plain/all-purpose flour

3 tablespoons vegetable oil

(or use 150 g/5 oz. filo/phyllo pastry)

FOR THE FILLING:

75 g/5 tablespoons butter

50 g/⅔ cup white or wholemeal/whole-wheat breadcrumbs

500 g/1 lb. 2 oz. apples, such as Granny Smith, Bramley or a mixture

grated zest of 1 lemon

1 teaspoon vanilla extract

50 g/¼ cup demerara/turbinado sugar

½ teaspoon ground cinnamon

½ teaspoon grated nutmeg

50 g/⅓ cup (Zante) currants (soaked in 1 tablespoon brandy, optional)

50 g/⅓ cup chopped almonds

1 tablespoon icing/confectioners' sugar

serves 6–8

To make the strudel pastry, sift the flour into a bowl. Combine 25 ml/1 tablespoon plus 2 teaspoons warm water and 2 tablespoons of the oil and stir it into the flour until you have a pliable, but not sticky, dough. Knead, then shape into a sausage. Taking one end of the sausage at a time, bash the dough onto a lightly floured work surface until small bubbles appear under the surface. This can take about 15 minutes. Knead it back into a ball and set aside, covered, for 30 minutes.

Preheat the oven to 200°C (400°F) Gas 6. To make the filling, heat the butter in a pan and gently fry the breadcrumbs until crisp. Peel and coarsely grate the apples, then add the lemon zest, vanilla extract, sugar, cinnamon, nutmeg, currants and almonds.

Roll the dough out on a lightly floured surface and shape into a rectangle. Brush it with the remaining oil. Stretch the dough to a paper-thin consistency by placing the knuckles of your hands underneath it and stretching it out. Alternatively, lay out the filo/phyllo pastry in a large rectangle, approximately 30 x 10 cm/12 x 8 inches.

Spread the apple and currant mixture over your pastry. Roll up the pastry with the contents, making sure to brush and seal both ends and the side with water. Brush the top with melted butter.

Bake for 30 minutes, or until crisp and golden. Sprinkle with icing/confectioners' sugar and serve hot or cold.

Types of Vanilla

'What does it mean to know the name of a thing whose nature one does not know'

George MacDonald, Scottish fantasy author

Of the 350,000 varieties of orchid, only one produces an edible seed pod. It is a tropical orchid that produces about 150 varieties of vanilla. The vanilla orchid is valued for its high vanillin content, and its rich and creamy floral notes are perfect when used in the dairy industry for ice creams, frozen yoghurts, custards and other flavoured products. Vanilla is also used extensively in the cosmetic and pharmaceutical industries, and as a food enhancer in the catering industry.

Technically, the majority of orchids are epiphytes, which means they need other plants to support their long vines. However, they also produce roots that trail along the forest floor, which thereby makes them terrestrial plants. Ancient vanilla plants would have grown on the ground. There is a misconception that the vanilla vine is a parasite, but it is not.

Only three types are commonly grown: *Vanilla planifolia*, *Vanilla pompona* and *Vanilla tahitensis*. The *Vanilla planifolia* species originated in Mexico and is the most extensively cultivated and available. It is more commonly known as Bourbon vanilla, but this has nothing to do with whiskey! It was given this name because it was grown in the Île Bourbon, the island southwest of Mauritius in the Indian Ocean, now known as Réunion. Bourbon relates to the European royal house of French origin and the island was named in their honour. Bourbon vanilla cuttings have been transplanted into many other vanilla growing regions, including Madagascar, which has built a reputation for producing the finest crop. There are several reasons for this, including Madagascar's unique biodiversity and favourable soil conditions. Once Bourbon vanilla became a viable cash crop, the curing process became more developed. The curing techniques for Bourbon vanilla varies depending on the location, but Madagascar has historically been regarded as the optimum place to grow and cure it. However, the arrival of modern technologies is changing this state of affairs.

Vanilla pompona is a variety originating from Guadeloupe and is indigenous around the Caribbean. It has less vanillin and shorter bean length and is not grown as a commercial crop.

Tahitian vanilla is the generic name for the *Vanilla tahitensis*. Tahitian vanilla began its evolutionary journey as a pre-Columbian Maya cultivar inside the tropical forests of Guatemala, but is thought to have cross-bred with *Vanilla pompona*. So why is it commonly referred to as Tahitian vanilla? According to Pesach Lubinsky, who has conducted pioneering research on the origins and domestication of vanilla: 'our DNA analysis corroborates what the historical sources say, namely, that vanilla was a trade item brought to Tahiti by French sailors in the mid-nineteenth century. The French Admiral responsible for introducing vanilla to Tahiti, Alphonse Hamelin, used vanilla cuttings from the Philippines. The historical record tells us that vanilla – which isn't native to the Philippines – was previously introduced to the region via the Manila Galleon trade from the New World, and specifically from Guatemala.' Tahitian vanilla has a completely different vanilla aroma with more floral and sweeter notes, as a result of the increased presence of floral heliotropin. It also has less vanillin content.

Puddings, Creams & Custards

Persian Rice Pudding

Some purists prefer their rice pudding to be a rice, milk and sugar only affair. But this Persian version (with its images of fields full of roses and of exotic spices) contains vanilla, which really brings an amazing range of complementary flavours together. Although this is served hot, you can enjoy it chilled as well. I can imagine eating it for breakfast.

50 g/3 tablespoons butter

100 g/½ cup arborio rice

850 ml/3 cups whole milk

100 ml/scant ½ cup cream (single/light or double/heavy, as you wish)

90 g/scant ½ cup caster/superfine sugar

1 vanilla pod/bean, split, seeds scraped and reserved

½ a cinnamon stick

grated zest of ½ orange

grated zest of ½ lemon

1 teaspoon rose syrup or 1 tablespoon rosewater

about 6 crushed pink peppercorns

a pinch of grated nutmeg

1 tablespoon flaked almonds (optional)

3–4 saffron strands/threads

1 tablespoon pomegranate seeds

2 tablespoons pistachios, roughly chopped

2 fresh figs, roughly chopped

serves 4

Preheat the oven to 140°C (275°F) Gas 1. Melt the butter in a pan over medium heat, then add the rice. Stir to coat the rice, as if you were making a risotto. Stir in the milk, cream, sugar, vanilla pod/bean and seeds, cinnamon, orange and lemon zest, rose syrup or rosewater, pink peppercorns, nutmeg and almonds, if using.

Transfer the contents of the pan to an ovenproof dish and bake for 2 hours; alternatively simmer it on the stove for 45 minutes, or until the rice is soft, making sure you stir it, especially towards the end of cooking. About 10 minutes before it is ready, stir in the saffron strands/threads.

Once the rice is cooked, garnish it with pomegranate seeds, pistachios and figs and remove the vanilla pod/bean before serving.

Lemon Syllabub

I recently attended a Tudor ball at the beautiful Bickleigh Castle in Devon. Not only was the event spectacular, but seated on my table was special guest and creator of Downton Abbey, Lord Julian Fellowes. Bickleigh's head chef, Scott Farr, did a superb job of researching and preparing a banquet fit for the occasion. It takes an experienced chef (Scott has been cooking for 30 years and owned his own restaurant before moving from London to Devon) to create a taste sensation that can transport you back to Tudor England. Tudor cuisine was known for being bland, with salt little used and spices very expensive, so a vanilla-infused lemon syllabub would have been a delight. It's no wonder then that when Queen Elizabeth I was first introduced to vanilla she adored it, and insisted on having it in everything for the last two years of her life.

8 lemons

400 g/2 cups caster/superfine sugar

500 ml/2 cups double/heavy cream

2 teaspoons vanilla extract

5 strawberries

serves 10

Finely grate the zest from the lemons, then cut them in half and juice them. Strain out any pips and add the juice to the zest.

Add the sugar to the lemon mixture. Pour half of it into a pan and heat gently to reduce to a syrup. Chill.

Whip the cream until it forms soft peaks. Fold in the remaining lemon mixture and the vanilla extract.

Pour the chilled lemon syrup into the bottom of 10 champagne flutes. Using a piping/pastry bag fitted with a large star nozzle/tip, pipe the syllabub into the glasses. Garnish with half a strawberry and refrigerate for 1 hour before serving.

LittlePod Custard

Custard is a must-have recipe in every household, and is fantastic, particularly with dishes like our Rhubarb and Strawberry Crumble (see page 97). We find that adding clotted cream gives the custard a lovely zing, as well as providing that little bit of luxury. Heaven from Devon!

100 g/½ cup golden caster/ raw cane sugar

1 teaspoon cornflour/cornstarch

250 ml/1 cup whole milk

125 ml/½ cup clotted or double/heavy cream

4 egg yolks, beaten

½–1 teaspoon LittlePod vanilla paste, or ½–1 vanilla pod/bean, (seeds only, see pages 8–9)

serves 4–6

Mix the sugar and cornflour/cornstarch together in a bowl. Whisk in the milk. Put the cream in a heavy-bottomed pan and heat it gently, slowly adding the milk mixture. Slowly bring it to the boil, stirring constantly, and reduce the heat when it starts to thicken.

Pour a little of the hot milk mixture onto the egg yolks, stirring well, then gradually stir this into the rest of the cream in the pan. Gently bring back to the boil and stir in the vanilla paste or seeds.

Serve immediately, or cover with clingfilm/plastic wrap to stop a skin forming, and reheat gently when needed.

To create flavour variations, try adding the finely grated zest of half an orange, a pinch of saffron or a tablespoon of toasted flaked/slivered almonds.

Vanilla Panna Cotta with Figs

When I was young my mother used to make this as a soother and reviver after I'd been ill, especially if I'd had a sore throat. The addition of the vanilla livens up what might otherwise be a rather boring pud. Any fruit works well with it, but my favourite is figs and honey.

2 gelatine leaves

a few drops of lemon juice

150 ml/⅔ cup whole milk

300 ml/1¼ cups double/heavy cream

110 g/generous ½ cup caster/superfine sugar

1 teaspoon LittlePod vanilla paste, or 1 vanilla pod/bean, (seeds only, see pages 8–9)

4 ripe, fresh figs

1 tablespoon clear honey

1 tablespoon Cointreau

½ a cinnamon stick

6 pink peppercorns

serves 4

Soak the gelatine leaves in a little cold water. Add the lemon juice to the milk and leave to stand for 10 minutes.

Pour the cream into a pan, add the sugar and cook over gentle heat, stirring, until the sugar has dissolved. Once it comes to a simmer, remove from the heat.

Stir the gelatine into the hot cream until it has dissolved. Strain it into a bowl and add the milk and vanilla paste or seeds. Divide the mixture between 4 small bowls or ramekins and refrigerate for at least 4–5 hours.

Meanwhile, preheat the oven to 200°C (400°F) Gas 6. Quarter the figs and put them in an ovenproof dish with the Cointreau, cinnamon stick and peppercorns. Bake for 20 minutes, or until tender. Stir in the honey and remove the cinnamon and peppercorns.

To serve, put the ramekins in very hot water for a few seconds, then invert them onto a serving dish. Serve with the baked figs.

Crème Brûlée

Crème brûlée sits well on any fine-dining menu, but its simplicity means that using good-quality ingredients is even more important. We're not short of good cream in Devon, and the vanilla? Well, we always have a little vanilla paste in our store cupboard! For extra flavour, decoration or both, you can always add your own twist, such as seasonal fruit, lavender or edible flowers.

30 g/2½ tablespoons caster/superfine sugar

6 egg yolks

600 ml/2½ cups double/heavy cream

1 teaspoon LittlePod vanilla paste, or 1 vanilla pod/bean, (seeds only, see pages 8–9)

2 tablespoons demerara/turbinado sugar

serves 4

Preheat the oven to 160°C (325°F) Gas 3. Put the sugar and egg yolks in a bowl and stir together. Put the cream in a heavy-based pan and stir in the vanilla. Bring to the boil over medium heat, stirring occasionally. Pour the cream onto the sugar and yolk mixture, stirring until well combined.

Divide the mixture equally between 4 heatproof ramekins. Place the ramekins on a baking sheet and fill it with water to come two-thirds up the sides of the ramekins. Bake for 30 minutes, or until set. Remove from the oven, allow to cool and refrigerate.

Spread the demerara/turbinado sugar evenly over the chilled ramekins, then place under a hot grill/broiler for 2–3 minutes until melted and bubbling. Alternatively, use a kitchen blowtorch to caramelize the tops.

Growing Vanilla

The vanilla orchid (*Vanilla planifolia*) grows wild on the periphery of tropical forests, 23 degrees either side of the Equator. It has thick, fleshy stems and small, greenish flowers. These flowers open early in the morning and release only a faint scent, without a trace of the vanilla aroma that we are familiar with. The flowers are pollinated by bees and hummingbirds.Once pollinated, the ovaries swell before transforming into fruits called 'pods' or 'beans', which are similar to long, thin runner beans (see the image on the right). They contain thousands of tiny black seeds.

Vanilla is the most labour-intensive agricultural crop in the world. The farmers who cultivate this plant need dedication and constant vigilance. The vine takes around 3½ years to flower, and requires a mycorrhizal fungus that naturally occurs in the soil, limiting where it will grow naturally. Two or three types of orchid bee traditionally pollinated the Mexican plants, but the bees died out and the process was eventually replaced by artificial pollination in Mexico, known as 'the marriage of vanilla'.

The discovery of this delicate operation was attributed in 1841 to a 12-year-old former African slave named Edmond Albius, who perfected the method on the Isle de Réunion. Belgian botanist Charles Morren had earlier discovered that small orchids need to be individually pollinated in order to fruit, and the Totanacs had known the secret of hand pollination, but it took Albius to share it. With the pointed tip of a bamboo stick, he lifted the thin, flap-like rostellum that divides the male anther and female stigma organs and pressed the pollen against the stigmatic surface. Success! A few days later, a vanilla pod/bean began to form. Even today, this is still the method for pollinating a commercial crop.

The vanilla flowers only last for one day, so it is a mammoth task to pollinate the flowers quickly. Hummingbirds, ants and other insects do act as pollinators, but would not be quick enough alone. It is a busy season that lasts for a couple of months, during which the whole community has to get out and hand pollinate. There are around 80,000 growers in Madagascar, and 1–3 kg/2–6½ lbs. of flowers are pollinated per day by just one worker.

From Plant to Table – the Curing Process

After pollination, the vanilla seed pods need to remain on the vine for at least 9 months, the length of a human pregnancy. The vines can be at least 30 m/100 ft in length, and some root stocks can last up to 1,000 years. Once the pods/beans have grown in length, it is best to harvest them before the seeds are too ripe. Then the real harvesting begins: the pods/beans are picked, gathered in and wrapped in wool. The four-stage curing process now starts.

First: killing the pod/bean by immersing it in hot water or, as in Mexico, using the sun. An enzymatic process begins, which promotes flavour.

Second: sweating, wrapped in paper or sacking in boxes. To prevent too much moisture building up, the pods/beans must be unwrapped every few hours to prevent them getting wet.

Third: drying. Only after five months of the curing process do the important glucovanillin/vanillin components start to emerge strongly.

Fourth: conditioning. The pods/beans have to be stored away from sunlight for some months, usually around 18 months altogether. Vanilla pods/beans reduce by 25–30 per cent of their original size during the curing process and this is when flavour is achieved.

Farmers fear leaving their pods/beans around for too long in case of theft, and often want to get on with the process too quickly. The industry has been threatened by lack of quality in the post-harvest process, and the amount of vanillin (which gives vanilla its unique aroma) in pods/beans has reduced over the years because of not exposing them to enough sunlight. Farmers need the incentive of a good price for their crop so that they are not tempted to cut corners.

Moreover, there are always threats from the environment. The Balinese plants were wiped out by a fungal disease called *Fusarium oxysporum*, which rots the root and spreads very quickly. It has been known to completely wipe out entire vanilla plantations in months. Unfortuantely, there is nothing that can be done after it appears in the plantation, which is why it's been referrred to as the 'scourge of vanilla'. Vanilla crops in Madagascar were also extremely hard-hit by Cyclone Hudah in 2000, which struck the northeastern part of the island. The cyclone destroyed half of Madagascar's vanilla crop, including 80 per cent of the plantations in Antalaha, the world's vanilla capital. Worse still, yet more devastating cyclones struck in the following years. This was the key contributing factor in the violent price fluctuations on the international vanilla market. In 1999, cured vanilla sold for around $50 a kilogram. By 2003, this had risen to $500. This led to two important changes; firstly, a number of new market entrants, like Uganda, India and Papua New Guinea attempted to take advantage of the now-extremely lucrative nature of vanilla. However, too many farmers had the same idea, and before long, the market was experiencing a glut in supply. By 2010, prices had dropped to $25 per kilogram – barely enough for farmers to survive on.

The second development that occurred post-2003 was vanilla importers' abandonment of natural or real vanilla in favour of synthetic alternatives, which now account for 95 per cent of the market. The painstaking care and hard labour that is involved in producing natural vanilla cannot be compared to the production of artificial vanillin. This process is reflected in the global production of 'real' vanilla. In a very good year, the combined world vanilla crop is around 2,300 metric tonnes. This may sound significant, but when compared to the 5 million containers of chocolate produced annually, or the 10 million containers of coffee, it does put the production of vanilla in context.

Brunch Dishes

Honey & Vanilla Granola

Granola is the ultimate wellbeing breakfast. It has become very fashionable, and you can, of course, vary the ingredients to include your favourites. On a recent late-summer visit to Portugal, apart from my delight at seeing LittlePod products on the shelves, I was entranced by all the trees bursting with nuts and fruit. It's an image I bear in mind when I eat my breakfast on a cold winter morning.

250 g/1 cup clear honey

1 teaspoon LittlePod vanilla paste, or 1 vanilla pod/bean, (seeds only, see pages 8–9)

450 g/3½ cups porridge/old-fashioned rolled oats

300 g/2¼ cups barley or millet flakes

50 g/½ cup soya/soy bran

½ teaspoon ground ginger

70 g/⅔ cup pumpkin seeds

70 g/⅔ cup sunflower seeds

70 g/1 cup rice puffs (brown or white)

90 g/⅔ cup chopped dried fruit, such as apricots, cranberries, figs, raspberries, or a combination

makes 30–40 servings

Preheat the oven to 120°C (250°F) Gas ½. Put the honey in a cup and stir in the vanilla paste or seeds. In a separate bowl, mix together the oats, barley or millet flakes, soya/soy bran and ginger together. Line a baking sheet with baking paper and spread out the granola mixture over it. Drizzle the honey mixture over the granola as evenly as possible, trying to cover it all. Bake for about 40 minutes, or until it is a light golden colour.

Tip the granola into a bowl and stir in the rest of the ingredients. Once cooled, store in an airtight jar. The granola should keep for at least 1 month.

Polenta Breakfast Bowl

Presenting polenta as an alternative to oats. Thinking of going out on a forced march after breakfast? Why not use the staple food of the Roman legions? More recently, polenta has been associated with northern Italy and is sometimes referred to as Italian grits. Enjoyed far beyond those borders now, polenta makes a fine porridge, as well as a very versatile base for many recipes. It was once eaten with salted anchovies and herrings — not for the faint-hearted at breakfast time!

250 ml/1 cup milk

80 g/⅔ cup quick-cook polenta/fine-grind yellow cornmeal

½–1 teaspoon LittlePod vanilla paste, or ½–1 vanilla pod/bean, (seeds only, see pages 8–9)

½–1 tablespoon soft brown sugar, plus extra for sprinkling (or substitute with sweetener of your choice)

extra warm or cold milk and fresh fruit, to serve

serves 3–4

Put the milk and 250 ml/1 cup water in a medium saucepan and bring to the boil. Reduce the heat to low, pour in the polenta/cornmeal and stir well.

Continue to cook gently, stirring frequently, for about 5 minutes (check the packet instructions for cooking times, as these can vary). When the polenta/cornmeal starts to thicken, stir in the vanilla and sugar to taste and continue to cook until the cooking time is up. If the polenta/cornmeal looks too thick, add an extra splash of water or milk to achieve the desired consistency.

Serve immediately in warmed serving bowls (polenta/cornmeal starts to set quite quickly), topped with a little more sugar and some fresh fruit. Pour over extra warm or cold milk, to your liking.

Apple & Blueberry Waffles

Waffles are a great breakfast or brunch treat, and this recipe is a refreshing diversion from the usual flavour combinations associated with them. Do not add too much fat, sugar or egg to the waffle mixture, or they will go soft soon after cooking.

FOR THE WAFFLES:

1 vanilla pod/bean

250 ml/1 cup milk

250 g/2 cups plain/all-purpose flour, sifted

2 teaspoons baking powder

½ teaspoon salt

½ teaspoon ground cardamom (optional)

2 tablespoons sugar

200 g/1 stick plus 6 tablespoons butter

250 ml/1 cup whipping cream

6 eggs, beaten

FOR THE TOPPING:

1 large apple

150 g/generous 1 cup blueberries

½ a cinnamon stick

1 star anise

2 whole cloves

300 ml/1⅓ cups pomegranate, grape or cranberry juice

vanilla yogurt and fresh fruit, to serve

waffle iron (optional)

serves 12

To make the waffles, split the vanilla pod/bean in half lengthways, then put it in a small pan with the milk, heat gently and set aside for at least 30 minutes. In a bowl, mix all the dry ingredients together. Melt the butter in a small pan. Add the butter and infused milk (discard the pod/bean), with the cream and eggs, to the dry ingredients and whisk lightly until a batter consistency is formed. Leave the batter to rest for around 30 minutes, or overnight in the refrigerator if possible.

Meanwhile, make the topping. Remove the cores from the apples and slice them, keeping the skins on. Place them, along with the other topping ingredients, in a pan and cook until the apple and blueberries are soft, about 3–4 minutes. Remove the fruit with a slotted spoon and set aside. Boil the remaining juices for 10–15 minutes, until a syrup consistency is reached. Strain the syrup to remove the spices, then return it to the pan to cook gently for a further 2 minutes, with the fruit. You can then blend the mixture if you like, or keep the fruit whole.

Heat a waffle iron over medium heat. Spoon the mixture into the iron, just up to the top. Cook the waffle until it is a golden colour, then remove and cool on a wire rack until ready to serve. To serve, pour the fruit over the waffles, adding a blob of something creamy, such as vanilla yogurt, and a handful of fresh red fruit.

Sweet Potato Pancakes with Cinnamon & Vanilla

Fiona Faulkner, mother and food writer, is passionate about getting children to eat fruit and vegetables, and has come up with many innovative recipes to help. This one is great because you can play Goldilocks and the Three Bears: a large pancake for Daddy Bear, a medium one for Mummy Bear and several little ones for Baby Bear.

300 g/10 oz. sweet potato, peeled and chopped

125 g/1 cup plain/all-purpose flour

1 teaspoon baking powder

1 teaspoon ground cinnamon

3–4 tablespoons caster/superfine sugar

1 tablespoon vanilla extract

125 ml/½ cup milk

1 egg, beaten

1 tablespoon butter, melted and slightly cooled

vegetable or groundnut oil, for frying

yogurt, stewed apples and maple syrup, or vanilla ice cream, to serve

serves 4–6

Bring a pan of water to the boil and steam the sweet potatoes until tender, then drain and leave to cool. Meanwhile, sift the flour, baking powder and cinnamon into a large mixing bowl. Stir in the sugar. Add the vanilla extract to the milk and egg, along with the melted butter. Gradually add the wet ingredients to the dry, combining it all together with a fork. The batter can be made up to 24 hours in advance and stored in the fridge in a bowl, covered, if you like.

Before cooking, mash the sweet potatoes, then stir them through the batter until well combined. Melt a little oil in a non-stick frying pan/skillet over fairly high heat. Once hot, carefully add heaped tablespoons of the batter. Gently fry until golden brown on both sides, turning them with a spatula.

Serve stacked with yogurt, stewed apples and maple syrup, either for a hearty breakfast that kids will love, or with vanilla ice cream for dessert.

Gluten-Free Chocolate Muffins

More and more people are experimenting with gluten-free products these days. Fortunately, all LittlePod products are gluten free, and these mouth-melting muffins were devised by our friend Barbara Freeman. They are delicious with ice cream, and coincidentally one of our customers, Razzle Dazzle, produces the perfect accompaniment in the form of their vegan ice cream, especially their Coconilla flavour. They concocted a beautiful red, white and blue knickerbocker glory for us during the Queen's Diamond Jubilee year.

150 g/10 tablespoons butter, softened

150 g/¾ cup caster/granulated sugar

2 eggs, beaten

90 ml/⅓ cup plus 1 tablespoon milk

1 banana, mashed

1 teaspoon vanilla extract

1 teaspoon LittlePod chocolate extract, or add a large tablespoon chocolate chips

100 g/¾ cup gluten-free flour

50 g/½ cup ground almonds/almond meal (if allergic, substitute gluten-free flour)

1 teaspoon gluten-free baking powder

½ teaspoon bicarbonate of soda/baking soda

1 tablespoon cocoa powder

50 g/⅓ cup chocolate chips

a 12-hole muffin pan with 12 small or 6 large muffin cases/liners

makes 12 small or 6 large

Preheat the oven to 190°C (375°F) Gas 5. Cream the butter and sugar together. Slowly add the eggs and milk, then add the banana, vanilla extract and chocolate extract (or tablespoon of chocolate chips).

Make sure the oven has reached temperature before continuing. Mix the flour, almonds, baking powder, bicarbonate of soda/baking soda and cocoa powder together, then add to the wet ingredients. Add the chocolate chips (or, if you like, add half the chips now and reserve half to sprinkle on top).

Fill the muffin cases/liners with the batter and bake for about 15 minutes for small ones or 20 minutes for large ones. Test by inserting a knife tip or cocktail stick into the centre of a muffin. If it comes out clean or with only a few crumbs, the muffins are cooked.

French Toast à la Vanilla

From the 'get-go' of Little Pod, our company has drawn together many talented young people, some of whom are still associated with us today. One such person is the talented artist and designer of our beer label, Harriet Beesley, who continually updates her diet blog on the LP website. She is convinced that the taste and smell of vanilla helps to stave off her sugar cravings. See page 83 for more about the extraordinary scientific research that may back up Harriet's claim!

2 UK large/US extra large eggs

a splash of milk

1 teaspoon vanilla extract

1 teaspoon olive oil

4 slices fresh thick white bread

1 lemon, cut into wedges

fresh berries and sugar, to serve

serves 4

Crack the eggs into a wide bowl, add the milk and vanilla extract and whisk it all together. Heat the oil in a frying pan/skillet over a medium-high heat. Dip the bread slices in the egg mixture and place them in the pan. Cook, turning the pieces over so they are golden brown on both sides. Serve with a squeeze of lemon, fresh berries, sugar to sprinkle and a lovely glass of freshly squeezed orange juice or your morning espresso – and relax!

Vanilla and Medicine

The indigenous Totonaca people used vanilla medicinally. The first reference to vanilla (not known by that name) was found in the Badianus Manuscript in the Vatican Library in Rome. The Badianus Manuscript, written in 1552, was a list of herbs used as medicines by the Aztecs, and was compiled by two Native American students at the College of Santa Cruz in Tlaltelulco, Martinus de la Cruz and Juannes Badianus. It was suggested that the vanilla plant be included in a potion to be worn around the neck to ward off infection. This was echoed by the writings of Dr. Francisco Hernandez, apothecary to King Charles II of Spain, who described how the Totonaca fashioned vanilla flowers into 'collars' to prevent various illnesses.

Up until the early years of the twentieth century, vanilla has been used as an antacid to calm upset stomachs. Its medicinal value was listed in the United States Pharmacopoeia – the authority regulating the sale of medicine and healthcare products – until 1916. It has been used to treat asthma, congestion and coughs. It has also been used as a sedative, for soothing burns and is used widely today in many pharmaceuticals and in cosmetic and aromatherapy products. The use of vanilla in wellbeing does have a scientific basis. Vanillin (the main component in vanilla) has been shown to activate A2-adrenoceptors: these enhance brain neurotransmitter release, which is involved in mood enhancement, pain reduction and an increased sense of calm.

An experiment was carried out in 1991 at the Sloan Kettering hospital in the USA into whether fragrances could help to soothe patients undergoing MRI testing. They found that heliotropin – one of over 250 known components in the make-up of vanilla – helped 63 per cent of patients endure the claustrophobic effects of MRI scans.

There is also a known compound in vanilla that is the nearest taste and smell to mother's milk. A study of 133 babies fed with breast milk or non-mothers' milk containing vanillin had a greater preference for vanilla-containing products as adults (Haller et al 1999, Chemical Senses vol. 24). Vanilla is also often used successfully to encourage nursing mothers to 'let down' their milk and also to encourage babies to latch onto their mother's breast when this has been problematic. It has been suggested that our predisposition towards vanillin is the reason why vanilla ice cream is the most favoured flavour in the world!

In St George's Hospital in London, UK, a dietician-led experiment held in 2000 drew a remarkable conclusion. The experiment involved attaching a vanilla-scented patch to the back of the hand. This proved to significantly reduce sweet food intake and led to greater weight loss compared with those wearing a lemon-scented dummy patch or no patch at all. The chief dietician, Catherine Collins, believed that the smell of vanilla could alter levels of the chemical messenger serotonin in the brain. We know that the smell of vanilla can last for up to 3 minutes in the nasal passages. Could that be long enough to resist temptation? The future should reveal more of vanilla's wellbeing secrets as the role of other compounds within vanilla begins to be understood.

It has been known for around 40 years that vanillin protects red blood cells infected with sickle cell disease from forming the characteristic sickle cell shape that blocks blood vessels. This had only been witnessed in test-tube experiments, because vanillin is broken down in the digestive tract before it enters the bloodstream. However, a 2004 study carried out at the Children's Hospital of Philadelphia synthesized a variant of vanillin, which had been chemically altered to resist degradation by the digestive tract. Promising results have led to a number of follow-up studies.

Vanilla has also been used for a variety of surprising medical and non-medical treatments. In certain parts of the world, it is used as a toothache remedy (vanilla dabbed directly onto the affected area), as an analgesic to relive menstrual pains and even as an insect repellant. A non-medical study suggested that it contains antimicrobial properties which means that it can prolong the life of food.

Desserts & Confections

Summer Berry & Sambuca Sabayon

This light and fruity sabayon is perfect for rounding off the vanilla-inspired fine-dining experience. We can imagine it being served up on a yacht off the coast of Italy. Despite its decadence, it's simple to make, looks impressive and can be enjoyed with Very Vanilla Shortbread (see page 13).

125 g/1 generous cup raspberries

125 g/1 generous cup strawberries, quartered

125 g/1 generous cup blackberries

125 g/1 generous cup white currants

12 UK large, US extra large eggs

100 g/½ cup caster/superfine sugar

75 ml/⅓ cup sambuca

1 tablespoon LittlePod vanilla paste, or 3 vanilla pods/beans, (seeds only, see pages 8–9)

icing/confectioners' sugar, to serve

serves 6–8

Rinse the berries in a colander, then drain on kitchen paper. Arrange neatly into each quarter of 4 shallow bowls or deep plates, allowing a gap between each section to pour on the sabayon mixture.

Separate the eggs. Place the egg yolks and sugar in a bowl over a pan of simmering water, whisk to combine and keep whisking until the mixture slowly but surely changes colour to pale yellow, almost white. After 5 minutes of constant whisking, slowly add the sambuca a little at a time. Whisk vigorously between each addition, until light and fluffy. Add the vanilla paste or seeds all at once and incorporate it evenly. Set the bowl aside somewhere warm.

Divide the sabayon equally between the bowls, adding a little to the top of each bundle of berries. Using a blowtorch, if you have one, toast the top of the sabayon to get a lovely, even golden colour throughout. Alternatively, place under a very hot grill/broiler for 1–2 minutes, or until golden. Be careful, as it can take a while to start browning, and will then change colour very quickly.

Dust generously with icing/confectioners' sugar and serve.

Rose Petal & Saffron Poached Meringues

Liz Knight is a food forager who uses Little Pod products in the lovely foraged herb mixes she sells to the likes of Fortnum & Mason and Selfridges. As she says, 'Once upon a time in Britain, roses were grown as much for their flavour as for their showy blooms, and fields were hued in purple saffron crocus flowers with their precious orange threads wafting in the breeze. British food has a heritage swathed in floral and botanical perfumes, flavours that blend with the sweetest of spices from the tropics: cardamom and vanilla.' This light-as-air pudding is a celebration of our British culinary heritage, made only better by the flavours wafting in from warmer lands. Serve to your loved ones and watch them look like the cats who got the cream as they lap the flavours up.

3–4 saffron threads

1 vanilla pod/bean, split, seeds scraped and reserved

25 g/2 tablespoons caster/superfine sugar

500 ml/2 cups single/light cream

4 egg whites

a handful of unsprayed rose petals, cut into fine strips (omit the white ends, which are bitter)

2 tablespoons roasted hazelnuts (or use cobnuts if you have them)

3 tablespoons unsalted pistachios

½ teaspoon rose petal preserve

serves 6–8

Place the saffron, the seeds from the vanilla pod/bean and 1 teaspoon of the sugar into a pan with the cream. Slowly bring the cream to a simmer, then take off the heat and leave to infuse for a couple of hours. (Saffron needs a little bit of time to allow the flavour to absorb into the cream.)

Meanwhile, whisk the egg whites until they start getting fluffy, add the remaining sugar and whisk to stiff peaks. Gently fold in the rose petal slices.

Return the cream to a low heat in a wide saucepan, and once it is steaming hot, spoon tablespoons of the meringue mixture onto the cream. Cover with a lid and poach gently until they are cooked through – about 5 minutes.

Chop the nuts briefly in a food processor. Pour the cream into a serving dish, top with the poached meringues, drizzle over a few dots of rose petal preserve and sprinkle with the nuts.

Sikarni

This recipe was kindly provided by Lalu Mahato, head chef at Nepal's Tiger Mountain Pokhara Lodge, which was opened by Edmund Hillary and is a favourite retreat for all those seeking peace and tranquillity in the heart of the Himalayas. It's great to know that Himalayan walkers and climbers are being treated to Little Pod vanilla-infused dishes. Sikarni is a spiced yoghurt suitable either as a breakfast or dessert dish. It was popular in the grand houses of the Rana family, erstwhile Prime Ministers of Nepal.

400 g/14 oz. Greek-style yogurt

1 teaspoon clear honey

1 teaspoon LittlePod vanilla paste, or 1 vanilla pod/bean, (seeds only, see pages 8–9)

½ teaspoon ground cinnamon

½ teaspoon ground green cardamom seeds

½ teaspoon saffron threads (optional)

a handful of pistachio nuts

serves 4

Pour the yogurt into a bowl. Add the honey and vanilla paste or seeds and stir together. Add the cinnamon and cardamom. If you like, soak a few threads of saffron in a little hot water or hot milk, strain and add to the yogurt mixture. Roughly chop the pistachios. If serving later, re-chill the yogurt.

Sikarni goes very well with Very Vanilla Shortbread (see page 13) or with Cadamom and Vanilla Cookies (see page 14).

Pineapple Carpaccio with Toasted Coconut & Lime Parfait

Masterchef alumnus, food consultant and restaurateur Peter Gorton, kindly donated one of his recipes to this book – a complex but rewarding dish reminiscent of a taste of summer in the Caribbean.

FOR THE CARPACCIO:

1 small, ripe pineapple

2 limes

120 ml/½ cup Malibu rum

525 g/2¾ cups sugar

½ tablespoon pink peppercorns

FOR THE PARFAIT:

600 ml/2½ cups double/heavy cream

juice and zest of 4 limes

2 vanilla pods/beans, split, seeds scraped and reserved

1 x 400-ml/14-oz. can coconut milk

12 egg yolks plus 5 egg whites

125 g/1 generous cup icing/confectioners' sugar

FOR THE TUILE:

2½ tablespoons butter

1 tablespoon grated orange or lime zest

225 g/1 cup plus 2 tablespoons caster/granulated sugar

75 g/⅔ cup plain/all-purpose flour, sifted

100 g/1 generous cup desiccated/shredded coconut (unsweetened), or 125 g/1 cup sesame seeds

6 egg whites

2 tablespoons milk

4 x 100–150 ml/⅓ cup moulds

serves 4

For the carpaccio, peel the pineapple and carefully remove all the hard knots with a sharp knife.Cut it into very thin slices and set aside in the fridge. Peel the zest off the limes and cut the zest into julienne strips. Squeeze and reserve the juice. In a saucepan, blanch the zest in boiling water for 30 seconds, then repeat 3 times. Dissolve 75 g/⅓ cup sugar in 60 ml/¼ cup water to make a syrup, add the lime zest and simmer gently until the zest is candied. Put 480 ml/2 cups water and the remaining sugar in another pan and bring to the boil, then remove from the heat, add the Malibu, lime zest, pink peppercorns and lime juice, then cool. Add the pineapple slices to the syrup and leave to marinate for at least 12 hours.

For the parfait, combine the cream, lime zest and vanilla seeds in a pan and bring to the boil over high heat. Immediately reduce the heat and simmer, uncovered, until it has reduced by a quarter, about 20 minutes. Remove from the heat and leave to cool, then refrigerate for at least 2 hours.

Reduce the coconut milk and lime juice by half, then set aside to cool. Strain into a bowl, mix with the cream and whip it to soft peaks. Beat the sugar and egg whites to make a sabayon in a heatproof bowl set over a pan of barely simmering water. Beat until pale, then leave to cool. When cold, fold it into the cream mixture and pour into the moulds (alternatively, you can use a loaf pan, lined with clingfilm/ plastic wrap (for ease of lifting out). Freeze until firm – at least 8 hours.

For the tuiles, preheat the oven to 170°C (325°F) Gas 3. Beat the butter with the citrus zest, add the sugar and mix well, then fold in the flour and coconut or sesame seeds. Fold in the egg whites gradually, adding the milk if needed. Spread the mixture out thinly on a baking sheet lined with baking paper and bake for approximately 8 minutes, or until golden and crisp.

To serve, place the pineapple slices on large plates, cover with a little syrup, add the parfait in the middle of the plate and top with a tuile. Serve immediately.

Tiramisu

The wonderful thing about vanilla is how it uplifts other flavours, one of which is coffee. My artist friend Gentian came to our local farm shop to demonstrate her own version of the classic tiramisu, and people loved it. She was passionate about using as many LittlePod products as possible, and the result is the gold standard recipe, as far as we're concerned.

400 g/1¾ cups mascarpone

1 teaspoon LittlePod chocolate extract (optional)

3 eggs, separated

60 ml/¼ cup Marsala wine

1 teaspoon LittlePod vanilla paste, or 1 vanilla pod/bean, (seeds only, see pages 8–9)

60 g/⅓ cup caster/superfine sugar

1 tablespoon LittlePod coffee extract, or 180 ml/¾ cup very strong coffee

4 tablespoons Amaretto liqueur or dark rum

about 18 Savoiardi biscuits/ladyfingers

grated chocolate or cocoa powder, to dust

serves 6

First, mix the mascarpone with the chocolate extract, if using. Whisk the egg yolks with the Marsala and vanilla paste or seeds until light and fluffy, then stir into the mascarpone. Separately, whisk the egg whites to stiff peaks and gently stir in the sugar. Gently fold the egg whites into the mascarpone mixture.

Mix the coffee and Amaretto or rum together. Dip each Savoiardi biscuit/ladyfinger into the mixture and make a layer of them in a serving dish. Spread approximately 1 cm/½ inch of the mascarpone mixture on top. Continue making layers, finishing with a layer of mascarpone mixture (the total number of layers will depend on the size of the dish you use).

Refrigerate for 6–8 hours, or until set. Before serving, dust with grated chocolate or cocoa powder.

Strawberry & Rhubarb Crumble

Imagine my shock to find myself eating a delicious fruit crumble (which I always associate with Britain), in a restaurant in Reims, France. Ever since then it's been my ambition to create a dish to rival theirs, and I think I'm just about there with this recipe!

4 medium sticks rhubarb

100 g/1 generous cup strawberries

1 tablespoon Calvados or brandy

grated zest of 1 lemon

1 teaspoon LittlePod vanilla paste, or 1 vanilla pod/bean, (seeds only, see pages 8–9)

1 teaspoon clear honey

230 g/1¾ cups plain/all-purpose or wholemeal/whole-wheat flour

120 g/1 stick butter

1 tablespoon rolled/old-fashioned oats

230 g/1 cup plus 2½ tablespoons demerara/turbinado sugar

1 tablespoon granola or muesli with nuts and fruit

½ tablespoon pistachio nuts, chopped

LittlePod custard (see page 58) or vanilla ice cream, to serve

serves 6

Preheat the oven to 200°C (400°F) Gas 6. Strip the rhubarb of any strings and cut it into 2.5-cm/1-inch pieces. Peel, core and slice the strawberries and gently cook them for 5 minutes in a saucepan with 2 tablespoons water. They need to soften a little, but not fully cook. Add the Calvados or brandy along with half the lemon zest and vanilla paste or seeds. Set aside while you make the topping.

Place the flour and butter in a food processor and whizz to a crumbly texture. Add the oats, sugar, granola or muesli and pistachios. Mix a little until the ingredients have combined into a good crumble mixture.

Place the fruit mixture in an ovenproof dish and spread the crumble topping evenly over it, pressing it down gently. Put a small piece of butter on top.

Put the dish in the oven and immediately reduce the temperature to 180°C (350°F) Gas 4. Bake for 30 minutes. If you like, spread extra demerara/turbinado sugar over the surface, then place under a medium-hot grill/broiler until caramelized to a golden-brown colour. Serve with LittlePod custard or vanilla ice cream.

Devon Vanilla Fudge

There is no fudge quite like Devonshire fudge. It's not clear how long it has been produced for, but we like to think that visitors to the county have enjoyed the treat since the time of Jane Austen. We believe it was a gift from America. To make it an extra special treat, use Devon clotted cream rather than double/heavy cream. Popped in a bag or box and decorated with ribbon, these make a lovely gift too.

350 g/1¾ cups caster/granulated sugar

80 g/5 tablespoons butter

150 ml/⅔ cup milk

150 ml/⅔ cup clotted or double/heavy cream

½ teaspoon LittlePod vanilla paste, or ½ a vanilla pod/bean, (seeds only, see pages 8–9)

30 g/2 oz. white chocolate, melted

makes 36 pieces

Cook the sugar, butter, milk and cream in a heavy-bottomed pan over low heat, stirring, until the sugar has dissolved and the mixture is creamy. Stir in the vanilla paste. Bring the mixture to the boil, stirring constantly. Boil for about 15 minutes, until it has a creamy, thick consistency. If you have a sugar/candy thermometer, it should reach 115°C (240°F).

Take the mixture off the heat and whisk it in a bowl or stand mixer to add that extra smoothness. This will take around 10 minutes. Halfway through, add the melted white chocolate.

Spread the cooled mixture into a small, greased baking pan or moulds and leave to cool for a few hours.

Champagne & Vanilla Chocolate Truffles

To cheer up a dull January evening I prepared a very special feast in our village for the Farringdon Society of Arts. I wanted to create a gathering with food as the centrepiece, and I love the fresh, spicy and simple approach that Yotam Ottolenghi embraces in his dishes, so I decided to write to him for inspiration. Not only did he send me some suggestions, he also told me this: 'I think your project is fantastic. I am particularly touched by the combination of art, agriculture and food in a real, living setting. I feel honoured to have been the culinary heart of your event.' After 12 different Ottolenghi-inspired dishes had been enjoyed, I topped the evening off with truffles enhanced with LittlePod vanilla. Prosecco will do, unless you happen to be opening a bottle of Champagne! We raise a toast to Yotam.

60 g/2 oz. milk chocolate

200 g/6½ oz. dark/bittersweet chocolate

40 ml/3 tablespoons brandy

150 g/10 tablespoons butter, cut into small pieces

80 ml/⅓ cup Champagne or Prosecco

1 teaspoon LittlePod vanilla paste, or ½ a vanilla pod/bean, (seeds only, see pages 8–9)

150 g/5 oz. dark/bittersweet chocolate (minimum 75 per cent cocoa solids), to coat

2 generous tablespoons cocoa powder, to coat

a 14-cm/5½-inch square baking sheet, lined with clingfilm/plastic wrap

makes 60

Chop both types of chocolate and place in a heatproof bowl set over a pan of barely simmering water until half melted. Heat the Champagne or Prosecco and brandy together in a pan until hot but not boiling. Stir it into the chocolate with a spatula, then stir in the butter. Add the vanilla paste and stir it in.

Spread the mixture into the baking sheet and refrigerate for 3 hours, or until set. Alternatively, pour the mixture into chocolate moulds, if you have them.

Using a sharp knife, cut the chocolate truffle mix into 2-cm/¾-inch squares, or roll into balls, if you like. Place the coating chocolate in a heatproof bowl set over a pan of barely simmering water and, once melted, remove from the heat. Using a couple of forks, dip each square into the chocolate, trying to keep any excess to a minimum, then quickly roll in the cocoa powder and transfer to a suitable serving dish. Store in the fridge, but remove and serve at room temperature.

Madagascar

'Madagascar is an unrepeatable experiment; a set of animals and plants evolving in isolation for over 60 million years. We're still trying to unravel its mysteries. How tragic it would be if we lost it before we even understand it'. **Sir David Attenborough, brodcaster and naturalist**

The Equatorial Belt, with its steamy tropical rainforests, is responsible for taking up a great proportion of the carbon dioxide that is released as a result of fossil fuel consumption today. In fact, along with the cool boreal forests in the high latitudes and the temperate forests of the mid-latitudes, they are thought to account for one third of the absorption of greenhouse gases.

Vanilla can be grown in many countries around the Equator, but the best soil conditions are thought to be in Madagascar. However, Madagascar is a prime example of an ecosystem under threat and its future, despite its distance from us, is very much linked to us and the choices we make in our kitchens.

Conservation issues and environmental threats, including deforestation, a growing population and lack of food security, are among the many forces currently having an enormous impact on this unique island.

Environmentalists have raised awareness of the importance of biodiversity in the natural world, making us aware that soil erosion, caused by deforestation, can wreak devastation and despair around our planet. It is thanks to them that we have the opportunity to do something about it.

In addition, from our school days we all know the important role that plants and photosynthesis play in regulating our climate. What we probably don't appreciate is the vast economic value that the cycle of photosynthesis contributes to the sustainability of life on earth. It is a service that money can't buy.

Why is this so important to the cultivation of the vanilla orchid, and why should we be concerned?

Humans have achieved much by harnessing photosynthesis, which enables us to cultivate stronger crops, extract nutrients and aid crop rotation. However, like the boom-and-bust effects of our global economy, this has not been without a cost. We all now face the greatest challenge for our generations, that is, how can we play our part in redressing the issues of climate warming and help to establish the right balance in the natural world.

These ecological problems may seem far away when you're in the kitchen with your apron on, wrestling with how to 'butterfly' slice your vanilla pod/bean to make your custard! But believe me, there is a connection. We are the end users in a production cycle that started at least five years ago, with a vanilla vine hugging its host tree in the tropical forest.

Beverages
& Ices

Lavender Hot Chocolate with Vanilla

We are very lucky to have a large, very colourful garden at LittlePod HQ, and every summer, the front garden is filled with lavender. We love the scent; which reminds us of sunny days and lunches on the terrace, and we also like to use it in our cooking. This hot chocolate is made with real chocolate rather than cocoa powder, and you can adjust the sweetness to your taste. The vanilla marshmallows are the equivalent of the icing on the cake!

FOR THE MARSHMALLOWS:

400 g/2 cups caster/superfine sugar

1 tablespoon golden syrup/ light corn syrup

4 tablespoons/¼ cup unflavoured powdered gelatine

2 UK large/US extra large egg whites

1 teaspoon LittlePod vanilla paste, or 1 vanilla pod/bean, (seeds only, see pages 8–9)

125 g/1 cup minus 2 tablespoons icing/ confectioners' sugar

FOR THE HOT CHOCOLATE:

480 ml/2 cups whole milk

½ teaspoon vanilla extract

½ teaspoon lavender flowers

80 g/2½ oz. milk or dark/bittersweet chocolate

a 23-cm/9-inch cake pan, lightly greased and dusted with icing/confectioners' sugar

serves 2 (makes 18 marshmallows)

Put the caster/superfine sugar, golden/light corn syrup and 175 ml/ ⅔ cup water in a small pan and cook over medium heat until it reaches 127°C (260°F); you can use a sugar/candy thermometer or test it by dropping a small amount of syrup into cold water – it is ready when it forms a rigid ball.

While the syrup is simmering, put the gelatine and 125 ml/½ cup water in a heatproof bowl. Place the bowl over a pan of barely simmering water and stir until the gelatine has dissolved, then keep warm until the syrup is ready. Remove the syrup from the heat and whisk in the gelatine mixture. Set aside.

In a separate large mixing bowl, whisk the egg whites to soft peaks. Carefully add the syrup mixture to the egg whites and keep whisking until they are very stiff. Stir in the vanilla paste or seeds, then spread out evenly in the prepared pan and leave to rest for at least 8 hours, ideally overnight, before cutting.

To make the hot chocolate, heat the milk, vanilla and lavender over medium heat, whisking occasionally, until the milk begins to simmer. Remove from the heat and let the lavender steep for 5 minutes. Strain to remove the lavender, then return the milk to the pan. Break the chocolate into pieces, add it to the hot milk and stir until the chocolate is melted and incorporated. Whisk the milk mixture for 10–20 seconds, until frothy, then serve topped with marshmallows.

Vanilla Lassi

No curry is really complete without a lassi, whether sweet or salty. This one is creamy and incredibly indulgent. Classic lassi flavourings include rosewater, mint, cumin, black pepper and cardamom, but chef and author Manju Malhi has created this refreshing vanilla lassi using our natural vanilla paste, and has even introduced it to her millions of followers in India.

100 ml/6 tablespoons single/light cream

200 ml/¾ cup whole milk

400 ml/1⅔ cups natural unsweetened yogurt

2 teaspoons LittlePod vanilla paste, or 2 vanilla pods/beans, (seeds only, see pages 8–9)

2 teaspoons sugar (optional)

freshly grated nutmeg, to serve (optional)

serves 2

Whisk the first 4 ingredients together with the sugar, if using, and serve chilled. Garnish with freshly grated nutmeg, if using.

For flavour variations, try adding one of the following, in addition to the vanilla: a small sprig of finely chopped mint, ¼ teaspoon ground coriander, ¼ teaspoon ground cumin, 6 chopped strawberries or ½ teaspoon rose syrup.

Eggnog

We love the word 'noggin', which means a small carved wooden goblet traditionally used to serve alcohol. If you thought it was an unassuming drink, you may want to reconsider: it caused a riot, known as the Eggnog Riot, at the United States Military Academy, in Christmas 1826, when cadets smuggled whiskey into their barracks to make the drink. Sadly, they were court-martialled. So think of these cadets when you toast your eggnog noggins this Christmas!

6 eggs, separated

250 g/1¼ cups caster/superfine sugar

180 ml/¾ cup good-quality brandy

700 ml/3 cups milk

¾ teaspoon grated nutmeg, plus extra to serve

½ teaspoon LittlePod vanilla paste or vanilla extract

450 ml/2 cups double/heavy cream

serves 4

Beat the egg yolks with the sugar for about 10 minutes, until the mixture is firm and buttery. Very slowly add the brandy. Refrigerate the mixture overnight, if possible, or for a good 6 hours.

Once sufficiently cooled, stir in the milk, nutmeg and vanilla paste or extract. Whip the cream with an electric mixer until stiff. In a separate bowl, beat the egg whites to stiff peaks. Gently fold the egg whites into the yolk mixture, then fold in the cream.

Serve in cups or glasses and sprinkle with extra nutmeg.

White Lady with Vanilla

Second only to Champagne, this is my all-time favourite alcoholic drink. Vanilla is not an ingredient in the classic version, but, loving vanilla as I do, I think it rounds out and deepens the flavour. To enhance your cocktail why not split a vanilla pod/bean (a used pod/bean is fine) and put it in a jar of sugar for two weeks or more, then use the sugar on the rim of your cocktail glass. Wet the rim of your glass with lemon juice and then dip into the sugar.

1 part good-quality gin

1 part freshly squeezed lemon juice

1 part Cointreau

½ a vanilla pod/bean or vanilla sugar

ice cubes

serves 1

Place the gin, lemon juice and Cointreau and vanilla pod/bean, if using, (split if you'd like the seeds to add some additional vanilla flavour to your cocktail) in a cocktail shaker with a few ice cubes. Shake very well with ice, remove the vanilla pod/bean, and serve in a cocktail glass. Alternatively, rub the rim of the cocktail glass with Cointreau and dip the top of the glass in vanilla sugar. Shake the excess off, then pour in the cocktail.

To create variations, try adding fresh lime juice instead of lemon, a sprig of fresh mint, a twist of orange peel or a dash of grenadine. Adding an egg white to the cocktail shaker will give it a more substantial texture.

The Lounger

We use either a light or dark rum for this, which has been infused with an unsplit vanilla pod/bean for 3 weeks or longer. Alternatively, you might want to decant however much rum you are prepared to spare for this recipe! The cherry or sugar is used to sweeten what is otherwise a cocktail for people who prefer their drinks without too much sweetness. The title incorporates the names of the ingredients, rather than referring to your likely activities after you've drunk a few, by the way.

1 part freshly squeezed lime juice

1 part vanilla-infused rum

1 part ginger cordial

¼ teaspoon sugar syrup (see method)

ice cubes

1 glacé/candied cherry (optional)

serves 1

To make the sugar syrup, put 2 parts sugar to 1 part water in a saucepan (the quantities depend, of course, on how much you want to make), and boil until the sugar has just dissolved. Leave to cool completely before using.

Measure the lime, rum, ginger and sugar syrup into a cocktail shaker. Add a couple of ice cubes, replace the lid and shake as if it were your boss's neck. Pour into a cocktail glass and add a glacé/candied cherry if you want a touch of extra sweetness.

Real Vanilla Ice Cream

From vanilla royalty comes the most regal of vanilla recipes. There is no substitute that can compare with real vanilla, and it is the most favoured ice cream flavour in the world. It is fitting, then, that we share this recipe, which was given to us by our friend, the inspirational Patricia Rain, the acknowledged champion of vanilla growers worldwide. Patricia was crowned Vanilla Queen by the vanilla farmers in Mexico, and we were thrilled when she agreed to attend our first anniversary tea party. Her support for, and understanding of, the aims and ethos of Little Pod is very important to us: sharing our knowledge and love of vanilla, and telling its story.

6 egg yolks

230 ml/scant 1 cup milk

200 g/1 cup caster/superfine sugar

1 vanilla pod/bean, split lengthways

450 g/2 cups double/heavy cream

1 tablespoon vanilla extract

a pinch of salt

makes 16 scoops

Put the egg yolks and milk in a heatproof bowl over a pan of barely simmering water and whisk until well blended. Stir in the sugar and salt and add the vanilla pod/bean, first scraping the seeds into the mixture. Continue to cook, stirring constantly, until the mixture is thick enough to coat the back of a spoon.

Cool the mixture, then cover and refrigerate until chilled. Remove the vanilla pod, stir in the cream, then add the vanilla extract.

Pour into an ice-cream maker and prepare according to the manufacturer's instructions. Once frozen, pack the mixture down and allow it to 'ripen' for about 2 hours before serving.

Vanilla Beer Ice Cream

In 2012, the Queen's Diamond Jubilee year, I was astonished and honoured to be awarded a British Empire Medal. In celebration, I decided to develop a LittlePod vanilla beer especially for our hampers. Lo and behold, the beer was selected by the Houses of Parliament's all-party beer society to accompany the coffee panna cotta at their chairman's dinner at the House of Commons. The following summer a local chef, Dez Turland, used it to create a vanilla beer ice cream, which is very satisfying on a hot day.

600 ml/2½ cups double/heavy cream

150 ml/⅔ cups whole milk

150 g/¾ cups light brown sugar

4 egg yolks

330 ml/12 fl. oz. LittlePod vanilla beer (or a vanilla-infused dark beer)

1 teaspoon ice-cream stabilizer

½ teaspoon LittlePod vanilla paste, or ½ vanilla pod/bean, (seeds only, see pages 8–9)

ice cream maker

makes 20 scoops

Put the cream, milk and sugar in a pan and heat gently until the sugar has dissolved, then pour it onto the egg yolks and whisk well.

Return the mixture to a clean pan, then cook over low heat, stirring constantly, until it thickens and coats the back of a spoon. Remove from the heat.

Put the vanilla beer in a pan and heat it gently to reduce by half. Whisk it into the egg mixture along with the ice-cream stabilizer and vanilla paste.

Allow to cool before transferring to an ice-cream maker, then churn according to the manufacturer's instructions. Transfer to the freezer for about 2 hours before serving.

Mythology of Vanilla

This is the legend of how the first vanilla orchid came to be:

Once upon a time, in the Land of the Good and Resplendent Moon, there was a kingdom ruled by the peace-loving and artistic Totanac people. The beautiful valley of palms and shimmering sands, which is now known as Vera Cruz, was visible from several locations. One was the home of the Papan Bird, called Papantla. Another was an ancient city built to honour the Huracan deity to pacify Tlaloc, God of the Storms. It was here, in this tropical rainforest, that the 'black flower' (the vanilla orchid) was first cultivated and cured, and from where Papantla became known as the 'city that perfumed the world'.

Long before the vanilla flower existed, a very beautiful young woman named Princess Tzacopontziza, which means 'Morning Star', lived in Papantla. Her father and mother were distraught that their beautiful daughter might one day have to be given away to be married. They decided that they would offer her instead to the cult of Tonoacayohua, the Goddess of Crops and Subsistence. Morning Star devoted her life cheerfully to the temple, taking offerings of foods and flowers to the Goddess. However, one day she was spotted by a handsome young prince named Zkatan-Oxga, which means 'Running Deer'. He immediately fell in love with her.

Every morning Running Deer would watch her from a distance until his heart could wait no more. He wanted to approach her and take her for his wife. His love outweighed the danger of being captured and killed. So one day, when the clouds were misty with rain and Morning Star appeared to gather her flowers and doves in the forest, Running Deer approached her and declared his love. Morning Star fell in love with the prince at first sight and they ran deep into the forest together.

When they reached the first mountain they encountered trouble. A terrifying monster spewed out fire from a cave, forcing the young lovers to seek a new direction along the road. Another blockade appeared in the form of the priests of Tonacayohua, who were out walking. About to explain their situation, Running Deer began to speak, but before he could utter a word the priests struck out and beheaded him. Morning Star, too, suffered the same fate.

With the hearts still beating, the priests cut them from their bodies and took them to the temple, placed them on a stone altar and offered the hearts up to the Goddess. Their bodies were disposed of in a deep ravine. In the very spot where the two were murdered, some days later the grasses where their blood was spilled began to dry out and shrivel away. Their death had brought about an omen of change. Not long afterwards, a bush sprang forth and within a few days grew very quickly and became heavily laden with thick foliage. Soon after, an emerald-green vine emerged from the earth, with delicate tendrils, fragile, elegant and sensual. One morning the people woke to an amazing sight, as tiny yellow-green orchids appeared all over the vine that resembled a young woman in repose, dreaming of her lover. As each flower died, slender green pods developed, releasing a perfume so intoxicating that it was offered to the Goddess. This was how the blood of a young princess created the birth of xanath (vanilla), the nectar of the Gods.

The two lovers had been transformed into a strong bush and a delicate orchid. They became a sacred gift to the Goddess, and from that time forth have remained a divine offering.

Vanilla and Vanillin

'Let the chemist experiment over his tubes and phials as he will, he can never devise anything in the way of imitation to compare with Nature's own handiwork; the secret formula for the delicate qualities of vanilla, which minister to taste and smell alike, cannot be wrested from her.'

Joseph Burnett, American flavour manufacturer

Although there is no real substitute for pure vanilla, there is unfortunately a synthetic or artificial form of vanilla, usually referred to as vanilla essence, which is cheap to purchase in the supermarket. This product does not come from a vanilla pod/bean, but is made from a byproduct of a petro-chemical used in the wood pulp industry. Unlike real vanilla, which has over 250 complex compounds, artificial vanilla has only one, vanillin, which gives us only the scent.

Historically vanillin was derived from the polymer lignin, a by-product of an environmentally-unfriendly wood-pulping process. Nowadays, the majority comes from the chemical synthesis of two petrochemical-related compounds: guaiacol and glyoxylic acid. A more expensive, rice-bran-derived biosynthetic product is also available and is classed as 'natural'.

Almost 95 per cent of the baking industry uses synthetically produced vanillins. They insist that customers want cheaper foods and that we cannot tell the difference when we eat cakes that contain artificial flavours. The companies that do use real vanilla must shout about it rather than keeping it as their secret ingredient.

Many people in the West have lost touch with the story of vanilla, and as a consequence, 90 per cent of the vanilla flavour used in foods is made up of synthetically produced vanillin, and that in turn has had an adverse effect on the farmers in the Equatorial regions.

We need to become more knowledgeable about real vanilla and find ways of helping the farmers, thereby helping to sustain the ecosystem that provides us with the precious crop.

Vanilla is the only commodity with an easily accessible, cheap imitation. As Patricia Rain (crowned the 'Vanilla Queen' by Mexican farmers) has explained, just a 1 per cent incursion into this artificial market could double the need for real vanilla worldwide.

What would this mean for the rest of the world? Well, the impact would be massive. If you notice the price of your consumables – whether food items such as cakes, pastries, puddings and ice cream, or cosmetics and candles, or even the price of your doctor's prescription – these can all be influenced by the price of vanilla. Many of those products may not even use natural vanilla, but the companies will use the excuse of a rise in raw commodities prices to push their own prices up.

This is where consumer awareness of real vanilla and its journey becomes important, so that we can ask the question of chefs and manufacturers: 'Do you use real vanilla?'

The vanilla market has a long history of boom and bust, but it is a slow food and requires long-term planning. Farmers need to be helped to understand that they do not need to stop planting just because one year the crop may not be so profitable.

There is a paramount need to stabilize the industry by offering natural vanilla products that can compete with the cheap artificial essences that adorn many supermarket and grocery-store shelves. We are proud to be making our contribution with LittlePod vanilla paste in a tube.

Savoury Surprises

'Spring to Summer' Salad

In Spring, we feel connected to the vanilla farmers as we harvest our earliest salad crops from the Little Pod garden. We use raised beds to get a good depth of richness in an otherwise red clay soil. Another reminder of Madagascar with its red earth! This dressing will add a little luxury to your salad and piquancy to your spring vegetables.

1 carrot

1 courgette/zucchini

10 cherry tomatoes

4 fresh basil leaves

1 sweet red (bell) pepper

1 smoked mackerel fillet, skin removed

1 tablespoon mixed sesame and pumpkin seeds

FOR THE DRESSING:

1 tablespoon olive oil

½ tablespoon agave syrup

freshly squeezed juice of ½ lemon

1 garlic clove, finely chopped

½ teaspoon chilli/hot red pepper flakes

1 teaspoon vanilla extract

serves 4

Top, tail and peel the carrot. Peel it into wide ribbons with a vegetable peeler (or use a mandolin if you have one), and do the same to the courgette/zucchini. Quarter the cherry tomatoes and finely slice the basil leaves. Cut the red (bell) pepper into thin strips. Put everything in a large mixing bowl and crumble in the mackerel fillet. Add the seeds and mix with salad servers.

To make the dressing, combine all the remaining ingredients in a small jug/pitcher and mix well. Pour this all over your salad and toss to coat everything in the dressing.

Serve with a chilled white wine. It's that easy!

LittlePod Winter Salad

It came as a great shock one recent summer to have a French guest taking photographs of my salads. Chloe had applied to do a two-month placement with LP and we had said oui. Moreover, she was smuggling the recipes back to her father in France and since returning has kept up our fine tradition of salad-eating. It must have been the vanillagrette which made all the difference. And now Chloe 'ne vanillaregrette rien'...

1 large beet(root), raw or cooked, grated

½ medium red cabbage, shredded

2 small shallots or 1 medium-sized red onion, very finely chopped

a handful of seedless raisins, washed

a handful each of roasted pumpkin and sesame seeds

1 medium orange, deseeded and cut into small segments

FOR THE 'VANILLAGRETTE' DRESSING:

2 tablespoons olive oil

2 teaspoons balsamic or cider vinegar

½ garlic clove, peeled and crushed

1 teaspoon freshly squeezed lemon juice

1 teaspoon clear honey

½ teaspoon LittlePod vanilla paste, or ½ a vanilla pod/bean, (seeds only, see pages 8–9)

a pinch of salt and freshly ground black pepper

serves 4–6

This recipe is ridiculously easy to make. Firstly, toss the salad ingredients together in a bowl.

Mix the olive oil and vinegar together with a spoon until blended well. Add the remainder of the dressing ingredients and mix again. Now drizzle a couple of tablespoons of the dressing over the salad, according to taste. I've always found that this salad is an excellent accompaniment to Cassoulet (see page 146).

Truffled Sweetcorn Chowder with Vanilla

The following recipes are from Little Pod's Scottish development chef, Dave Buchanan. Dave has spent the last few years cooking on superyachts and in the kitchens of the rich and famous. But wherever he is, in his culinary toolkit, you'll always find Little Pod products. He's used vanilla from all over the world, yet insists that using vanilla paste is the way forward for the modern chef. Dave has kindly contributed a fine dining menu for this book.

1 large onion, finely diced

1 garlic clove, peeled and crushed

2 tablespoons vegetable oil

800 g/4½ cups sweetcorn/corn kernels (fresh, frozen or canned)

1 litre/4 cups chicken stock

125 ml/½ cup white wine

560 ml/2⅓ cups double/heavy cream

2 vanilla pods/beans, split and deseeded

truffle oil, to serve

a few fresh chives, finely chopped

oven-baked crostinis (optional)

salt and freshly ground black pepper

serves 6–8

Sweat the diced onion and garlic in a frying pan/skillet with the vegetable oil over a medium heat for 4–5 minutes. Make sure that the onion does not colour.

Add the sweetcorn/corn kernels, season and continue cooking over a medium heat for about 5 minutes.

Add the chicken stock, white wine and double/heavy cream along with the vanilla pods/beans and seeds. Bring to the boil and then turn the heat down to a simmer for 30 minutes, stirring occasionally with a wooden spoon. Turn the heat off and remove the vanilla pods/beans.

Carefully blitz the soup with a stick blender.

To serve, drizzle a little truffle oil over the top and finish with some finely chopped chives or some oven-baked crostinis.

Butternut Squash Soup

I'm sure everyone knows Fortnum & Mason in London, so you can imagine how thrilled we were when they decided to stock our products. I love to perform demonstrations there and once cooked alongside their house chefs. Armed with squashes from my garden, I confidently made my soup, but they looked on suspiciously as I squeezed in my vanilla paste. The result, however, was a triumph — the transformative effect of vanilla won the day.

1 medium butternut squash

a knob/pat of butter

2 teaspoons vegetable or groundnut oil

1 red onion, peeled and diced

1 medium potato, peeled and diced

1 large carrot, peeled and diced

1 medium parsnip, peeled and diced

560 ml/1 pint chicken or vegetable stock

a sprig of fresh thyme or sage

¼ teaspoon LittlePod vanilla paste, or ¼ of a vanilla pod/bean, (seeds only, see pages 8–9)

1 tablespoon fresh sage (optional)

herb or garlic bread, to serve

serves 4–6

Either: roast the squash in the oven at 180°C (360°F) Gas 4 for around 40 minutes until soft, then skin the squash and mash it into a purée with a little butter. Set aside. Alternatively, peel the squash, cut it into chunks and boil until soft, before draining and puréeing with butter. Set aside.

Meanwhile, heat the oil in a frying pan/skillet over a medium heat. Once hot, sweat the onion and potato for 3–5 minutes, but be careful not to brown them. Add the carrot and parsnip and cover with stock. Season to taste and add chopped sage or thyme. Simmer for about 20 minutes or until soft. Then liquidize the mixture in a blender.

Add the set-aside squash to the liquidized mixture and add the vanilla paste or seeds. Heat in a saucepan and garnish with the sage, if using, before serving. This soup goes well with a good chunk of herb or garlic bread.

Fillets of Sea Bass with Vanilla Sauce

One of the joys of being part of Little Pod is the constant connection we make with the most wonderful chefs and home cooks who delight in using real vanilla. We think it is the natural calmatives and uplifters that draw them towards it. This is a dish inspired by a wonderful recipe belonging to Michael MacDonald, chef-owner of Marlow's Vanilla Pod restaurant – one of the The Times top 100 UK restaurants.

200 g/7 oz. white cabbage, thinly sliced

a knob/pat of butter

200 ml/¾ cup white wine

560 ml/1 pint fish stock

2 potatoes, cut into thin discs

200 ml/¾ cup olive oil, plus 2 tablespoons for frying

4 large sea bass fillets

a pinch of salt and freshly ground black pepper

steamed asparagus, to serve

FOR THE VANILLA SAUCE:

½ a vanilla pod/bean, including seeds

2 tablespoons vegetable or groundnut oil

6 shallots, sliced

275 ml/½ pint white wine

275 ml/½ pint fish stock

275 ml/½ pint single/light cream

a pinch of salt and freshly ground black pepper

serves 4

Preheat the oven to 160°C (325°F) Gas 3.

For the vanilla sauce, cut the pod/bean in half, remove the seeds and put them to one side. Meanwhile, heat 2 tablespoons of vegetable or groundnut oil in a frying pan/skillet over a medium heat. Once hot, add the shallots with the ½ vanilla pod/bean, then season and add the white wine. Reduce to a glaze. Add the fish stock and reduce by half. Then, add the cream and bring to the boil. Adjust the seasoning to taste. Place the set-aside vanilla seeds in a sieve/strainer positioned over a bowl and pour the sauce through the sieve/strainer and into the bowl, to remove the shallots. Add the ½ vanilla pod/bean directly to the bowl, cover with clingfilm/plastic wrap and transfer to the refrigerator to infuse for up to 6 hours.

Sweat the cabbage in butter for 5 minutes until almost tender. Season, add the white wine then reduce by half. Add half the fish stock and braise until tender.

Lay the sliced potatoes in a ring. Pour over the remaining fish stock, olive oil and seasoning. Cook in the preheated oven for 10–15 minutes until tender.

Score the skin side of the sea bass fillets several times and season both sides. Heat a large frying pan/skillet until really hot, then add 2 tablespoons of olive oil. Lay the fish fillets in the pan/skillet (you may need to do this in 2 batches), skin-side down. As soon as the fillets go in, press each one down with your fingers or a fish slice to stop it from curling up. Reduce the heat to medium, and leave the fish to cook for 3–4 minutes, until the skin is crisp and brown. Carefully turn the fillets over, then fry on the other side for another 2 minutes. Meanwhile, remove the sauce from the refrigerator and reheat, stirring constantly.

Serve the potatoes in a little ceramic pot and cabbage on the side of the fish fillets. Garnish with the steamed asparagus and pour on the vanilla sauce.

Hand-dived Scallops with Vanilla Risotto and Pea Shoots

Vanilla goes really well with fish and seafood as demonstrated in this scallop risotto by Dave Buchanan. If you're looking for a recipe to impress your friends, try this one.

1 litre/quart chicken stock

2 vanilla pods/beans

4 hand-dived scallops in shell, shirked and cleaned (reserve corals – the curved orange part – for the sauce)

a knob/pat of butter

1 tablespoon olive oil

1 small white onion, diced

200 g/1 cup carnaroli rice

250 ml/1 cup white wine

50 g/⅔ cup grated Parmesan

120 ml/½ cup white port

560 ml/1 pint fish stock

560 ml/1 pint single/light cream

1 bay leaf

1 star anise

1 teaspoon LittlePod vanilla paste, or 1 vanilla pod/bean, (seeds only, see pages 8–9)

sunflower or unrefined sesame oil

sea salt and freshly ground black pepper

olive oil

a handful of pea shoots

serves 4

Simmer the chicken stock gently and add two split vanilla pods/beans. Remove from the heat and allow to infuse (overnight is best, but a few hours is fine).

Prepare the scallops and remove all of the skirt and trim. Dry them on paper towels.

To make the risotto, add a knob/pat of butter and a generous splash of olive oil to a frying pan/skillet. Soften, but do not colour, the onions for around 5 minutes. Add the rice and constantly stir until it turns shiny, about 2 minutes. Slowly add the white wine and then the set-aside chicken stock over a 20–30 minute period, stirring repeatedly until the risotto is fully cooked. Add the Parmesan.

For the sauce, reduce the port, fish stock and cream in a saucepan with the bay leaf, star anise and vanilla paste or seeds. Bring to the boil, then reduce to a simmer and add the scallop corals. Cook for a further 5 minutes. Blitz the sauce with a stick blender and pass through a fine sieve/strainer into a pan. Re-aerate the sauce with the blender just before serving.

Oil the scallops with sunflower or unrefined sesame oil and season. To cook the scallops, get a non-stick frying pan/skillet really hot, until it is smoking. Place them into the pan/skillet presentation-side down (that's the slightly larger of the two sides). Allow to cook for about 90 seconds (times vary depending on scallop size) take off the heat, turn the scallops and cook each for a further 90 seconds. Season lightly with some crushed sea salt.

To plate up, place the risotto on the middle of the plate, pop the scallop on top, and fill the base of the serving bowl with the light, aerated sauce. Drizzle a little olive oil around the plate and garnish with the pea shoots on the side.

Serve with a chilled Sauvignon Blanc or a nice glass of Billecart-Salmon Champagne for indulgent, decadent dining.

Honey and Vanilla Glazed Salmon

Vanilla can be used to make fantastic marinades for fish dishes. Incidentally, vanilla is also a great deodorizer – some fishermen even use it on their hands to disguise the odours they pick up during a day's work! On a related note, LittlePod's Tom has converted his dad, a devoted Devon fisherman, to using vanilla paste in many of his fish dishes...

2–4 fresh salmon steaks

2 teaspoons olive oil

1 teaspoon clear honey

1 teaspoon LittlePod vanilla paste, or 1 vanilla pod/bean, (seeds only, see pages 8–9)

pinch of salt and freshly ground black pepper

½ teaspoon finely chopped ginger (optional)

serves 2–4

Make a glaze by combining all of the ingredients except the fresh salmon steaks.

Brush the mixture evenly over the salmon and leave for at least 1 hour, or preferably overnight, in the refrigerator.

Place the fish under a hot grill/broiler for around 10 minutes until the glaze forms a crust and the fish is cooked through but still moist.

Serve with a pea shoot or watercress salad and a couple of wedges of lemon.

Manju's Coconut and Vanilla Chicken Curry

This recipe, our editor's choice in fact (!), has been included because Manju Malhi is a great friend of Little Pod and has been experimenting widely with our vanilla in Indian cuisine for her own cookbooks. I teach Manju how to make afternoon tea scones and she shows me which spices to grind in the mortar and pestle she gave me. Coconut is yet another great partner for vanilla.

2 tablespoons vegetable or rapeseed oil

1.5 kg/3½ lbs. of chicken pieces, at room temperature

1 medium onion, finely chopped

150 ml/⅔ cup chicken stock

1 teaspoon LittlePod vanilla paste, or 1 vanilla pod/bean, (seeds only, see pages 8–9)

75 ml/⅓ cup coconut milk

125 g/1 cup roasted cashew nuts, roughly chopped

coriander/cilantro, chopped, to garnish

basmati rice, to serve

FOR THE AROMATIC SAUCE MIX:

4 black peppercorns

4 cloves

1 star anise

½ teaspoon fennel seeds

3 dried red chillies/chiles

3 green cardamom pods

½ teaspoon poppy seeds

1 cinnamon stick

¼ teaspoon ground turmeric

serves 4

To make the aromatic sauce, heat a heavy-bottomed frying pan/skillet and add the peppercorns, cloves, star anise, fennel seeds, red chillies/chiles, cardamom, poppy seeds and cinnamon. Roast for 1 minute and then, adding the turmeric, grind to a powder either in a mill or a mortar and pestle.

Heat the vegetable or rapeseed oil in a frying pan/skillet and lightly brown the chicken pieces over a medium heat for 4–5 minutes. Set the chicken to one side, keeping warm. Then, add the onions to the pan/skillet and cook through until translucent but not coloured. Add a teaspoon of the aromatic sauce mix, stir well (reserve the rest for another time) and continue to cook for 2 minutes. Add the chicken stock, vanilla paste or seeds and coconut milk and bring to a simmer. Add the set-aside chicken and cook for another 20–30 minutes. Remove from the heat and strain the liquid. Combine the remaining liquid, chicken and cashews and reheat. Garnish with coriander/cilantro before serving with basmati rice.

Guinea Fowl with Ballotine of Leg Filled with Vanilla and Chicken Mousse

This is a very special recipe. It's the signature dish at Angela's restaurant in Exeter, our local city. Devon is well-known for hunting, shooting and fishing, alike. This recipe is a game enthusiast's delight and a perfect seasonal dinner dish.

whole fresh guinea fowl, about 1.3 kg/3 lbs.

100 g/3½ oz. skinless chicken breast

1 teaspoon dried thyme

1 egg white

60 ml/¼ cup whipping cream

20 g/2½ tablespoons fresh thyme leaves

2 teaspoons LittlePod vanilla paste, or 2 vanilla pods/beans, (seeds only, see pages 8–9)

extra virgin olive oil

a few fresh thyme sprigs

1 tablespoon chopped flat-leaf parsley

salt and freshly ground black pepper

FOR THE SAUCE:

500 ml/2 cups water

50 g/⅓ cup onion, chopped

50 g/⅓ cup carrot, chopped

50 g/⅓ cup celery, chopped

75 g/2½ oz. mixed wild mushrooms, diced

50 ml/3 tablespoons Madeira wine

serves 4

To prepare the ballotines, bone the fowl with a sharp knife; you require the breast whole and the thigh part of the leg with thigh bones removed. Pop the prepared guinea fowl in the bottom of the refrigerator. Set aside the rest of the carcass.

Using a food processor, blend the white chicken meat with the thyme and egg white until smooth .Then, gradually add cream to create a mousse. Remove from the food processor and place in a mixing bowl. Add the vanilla paste or seeds and fold into the chicken mousse mixture. Chill in the refrigerator for 1 hour.

Remove the chicken from the refrigerator. Using a palette knife, cover the inside of the thigh meat with 70 g/2½ oz. of chicken mousse, then roll the thigh into a log and season with salt and pepper then wrap tightly in clingfilm/plastic wrap. Steam the thighs in a stainless steel steamer for 10–15 minutes until cooked. Remove from the steamer and cool immediately in ice cold water. Once cooled, remove from the clingfilm/plastic wrap.

To make the sauce, place the guinea fowl carcass in a large saucepan and cover with water, add the chopped vegetables and bring to the boil, skim the top with a slotted spoon and reduce the stock to half its original volume. Strain the stock and reduce again until golden. Add the diced wild mushrooms and Madeira wine to the sauce and reduce it even further to make a jus. Keep warm until you're ready to serve.

Preheat the oven to 180°C (360°F) Gas 4.

Warm a roasting pan with extra virgin olive oil and scatter a few thyme sprigs. Season the breast and ballotine of guinea fowl with salt and pepper and place skin-side down in the tray. Cover with more olive oil and roast in the preheated oven for 15 minutes until golden and cooked through.

Place the breast on the plate, and serve with three evenly cut slices of the ballotine. Spoon over the reheated sauce. Serve with steamed leeks and trimmed baby carrots and scatter the parsley on top.

Lalu's Pork Sekuwa

This is a typical Nepalese snack served before a meal as 'Tippan Tappan' (nibbles). The addition of vanilla adds a mellow roundedness to the rich spices. This is Nepal's answer to tandoori pork tikka.

2 garlic cloves, peeled and crushed

1 small red onion, peeled and finely chopped

1–2 small green chillies/chiles, deseeded if a less fiery result is desired

1 teaspoon freshly squeezed lemon or lime juice

1 tablespoon olive oil

2 tablespoons Greek-style yogurt

salt and freshly ground black pepper, to taste

600 g/1 lb. 5 oz. lean pork, diced into 2-cm/¾-inch cubes

1 teaspoon LittlePod vanilla paste, or 1 vanilla pod/bean, (seeds only, see pages 8–9)

fresh coriander/cilantro, to garnish

serves 4

First make a marinade by mixing together all ingredients except the pork and vanilla.

Rub the vanilla paste or seeds into the pork cubes and leave to rest for 30 minutes, turning and rubbing occasionally; then place in the marinade for at least 2–3 hours.

Thread the pork cubes onto skewers and place under a hot grill/broiler for 20 minutes.

Garnish with fresh coriander/cilantro and serve hot. Serve with either 'Spring to Summer' Salad (see page 127) or LittlePod Winter Salad (see page 128), depending on the season.

Cassoulet

I love using a slow cooker – it is such a convenient and cost-effective way of feeding the family, especially if its members are in and out at different times. A hot one-pot meal is a great idea, particularly on those cold days. I made this cassoulet for a live music event held in my village and everyone was talking about the depth of flavour in the stock. By simply rubbing the paste into the duck breast, searing in the sweetness of the duck, the slow cooking did the rest.

1 medium potato

3 medium onions plus 1 for the stock

1 celery stick/rib

1 leek

4 garlic cloves, plus 1 for the stock

560 ml/1 pint chicken stock or water

1 small duck

1 teaspoon LittlePod vanilla paste, or 1 vanilla pod/bean, (seeds only, see pages 8–9)

500 g/1 lb. neck fillet of lamb

225 g/8 oz. whole garlic sausage, cut into chunks

2 tablespoons plain/all-purpose flour

350 g/12 oz. streaky bacon

4 tablespoons tomato purée/paste

275 ml/generous 1 cup dry white wine

bouquet garni

225-g/8 oz.-can haricot/navy beans

4 carrots, par-boiled

a dash of Worcestershire sauce

salt and freshly ground black pepper

slow cooker (optional)

serves 6–8

Switch on the slow cooker or preheat the oven to 180°C (360°F) Gas 4.

To make the stock, chop and sauté the potato, 1 onion, the celery stick/rib, leek and garlic. Add the chicken stock or water. When cooked, use a blender to create a base stock (as you would when making a soup). Pop into a slow cooker or earthenware pot.

Prepare the meat. Quarter the duck and separate the breasts. Rub the vanilla paste or seeds into the duck breasts and leave to marinate. Chop the lamb and spicy sausage into chunky pieces. Toss the duck legs and lamb fillet into the flour, with a little seasoning added in.

In a large frying pan/skillet, cook the bacon (grill/broil beforehand if you prefer), then gradually add the lamb and duck meat (minus duck breast) to sear and then set aside. Use the same pan/skillet to sear the duck breast then set aside as well. Then, cook the remaining onion and garlic and add tomato purée/paste and wine. Add the bouquet garni and reduce until thicker. Add the beans, carrots and the Worcestershire sauce.

Combine everything into your slow cooker, or if you're cooking it in the oven, in an earthenware pot, and season to taste. Cook for 1 hour in the preheated oven (or, if using a slow cooker, until the meat is tender).

Accompany with your favourite crusty loaf or potato dish.

Steak with Red Wine and Vanilla Jus

Dave's dish of the day (as in 'he likes it' rather than he is 'dish of the day'). A great way to cook steak, served alongside a succulent potato dish and topped off with a lovely sauce.

750 g/1⅔ lbs. potatoes

4 medium slices smoked bacon or pancetta

100 g/7 tablespoons butter

4 tablespoons crème fraiche or sour cream

1 tablespoon grated Parmesan

2 tablespoons chopped fresh rosemary

olive oil

4 sirloin/New York strip steaks (or other cut if you prefer)

2 teaspoons LittlePod chocolate extract (optional)

sea salt and freshly ground black pepper

1 shallot or red onion

350 ml/1½ cups red wine

1 bay leaf

600 ml/2½ cups chicken or beef stock (home-made is preferable)

½ teaspoon LittlePod vanilla paste, or ½ vanilla pod/bean, (seeds only, see pages 8–9)

salt and freshly ground black pepper

serves 4

Peel the potatoes and cut into quite thick slices before parboiling, draining and drying them. Place a layer of bacon or pancetta in an ovenproof dish and then layer the potatoes, with a tablespoon of crème fraiche or sour cream with a couple of knobs/pats of butter on top, followed by another layer of potatoes topped with chopped rosemary and salt and pepper to taste. Drizzle over some olive oil and sprinkle a little grated Parmesan on top.

Rub 2 tablespoons olive oil (mixed with the chocolate extract if you are using it) into the steaks. Sprinkle the steaks with a generous amount of sea salt. Place under a very hot grill/broiler and, depending on the thickness of the cut, cook for 2–3 minutes per side (a tip for sirloin steaks: using a scrunched up tube of aluminium foil, angle the steak with the fatty edge highest; this way the fat runs into the meat when cooking and keeps it moist). Rest for a few minutes before serving.

Heat up a tablespoon of olive oil in a frying pan/skillet and caramelize the shallot or red onion. Add the wine and bay leaf and bring to the boil, then turn down to a simmer until reduced by half. Add the stock and vanilla paste or seeds and reduce by half again. Strain the stock and reheat in the pan. Stir in a knob/pat of butter.

Serve with some fresh green vegetables.

Venison Loin in Vanilla Marinade with Chocolate Red Wine Sauce

The combination of vanilla and chocolate was first explored by the Aztecs in the 1500s. They created a hot chocolate and vanilla drink, known as 'xocolatt', which was subsequently discovered by the Spanish soldiers who referred to it as 'the divine drink which builds up resistance and fights fatigue'!

1 half loin of venison (around 650 g/1½ lbs.), with the silverskin (connective tissue) removed

1 tablespoon vegetable oil

1 bulb/head garlic

4 sprigs fresh rosemary

2 teaspoons LittlePod vanilla paste, or 2 vanilla pods/beans, (seeds only, see pages 8–9)

350 ml/scant 1½ cups red wine

1 litre/quart game/chicken stock

1 onion, chopped

1 carrot, chopped

4 stalks/ribs celery, chopped

1 bulb fennel, chopped

1 vanilla pod/bean

60 g/2 oz. good quality chocolate (70% minimum cocoa solids), chopped

1 tablespoon LittlePod chocolate extract, or, alternatively, add another 20 g/¾ oz. dark/bittersweet chocolate

600 g/1¼ lbs. sweet potatoes

pinch of grated nutmeg or cinnamon

16 medium asparagus spears

salt and freshly ground black pepper

serves 4–6

Marinade the venison overnight in vegetable oil with the split bulb of garlic, 2 sprigs fresh rosemary and 1 teaspoon vanilla paste or seeds. You can either cut the venison into steaks or leave it whole for cooking and carving later. I prefer leaving it whole.

To make the sauce, put the wine, stock and vegetables in a saucepan, add the remaining rosemary and the vanilla pod/bean. Bring to the boil and reduce to a simmer, reducing most of the liquid so you end up with a rich, reduced fragrant sauce. To finish the sauce, add the chocolate, chocolate extract (if using), remaining vanilla paste or seeds, and a knob/pat of butter and stir well. Pass the sauce into a clean saucepan through a fine sieve/strainer and cover with clingfilm/plastic wrap to keep warm.

Peel and roughly chop the sweet potatoes and boil in salted water until tender, about 20 minutes. Pass them through a fine sieve/strainer until you have a smooth purée and adjust the seasoning. Add a knob/pat of butter, mix well and spoon into a disposable piping bag for later.

Peel the asparagus spears and remove the woody end. Reserve the trims for the stock. Boil them in heavily salted water for about 3 minutes and refresh in ice cold water.

Remove the venison from the refrigerator and allow to come to room temperature before cooking. Meanwhile, preheat the oven to 240°C (465°F) Gas 9. Get a heavy-bottomed, ovenproof frying pan/skillet really hot, until it starts to smoke. Add the loin and fry for 4 minutes on one side. Turn over and place the frying pan/skillet into the preheated oven for about 4 minutes. Remove from the oven and allow to rest on a cooling rack. Toss the asparagus spears back into the venison pan to warm them through and take on some flavour.

To serve, reheat the sauce, carve fairly thick slices of the venison at a 45° angle and place on each plate. Slip a few asparagus spears alongside the venison, add a serving of sweet potato and finish with a good drizzle of the sauce.

Vanilla in Crisis

'The world is too much with us; late and soon,
Getting and spending we lay waste our powers:
Little we see in nature that is ours...' **William Wordsworth**

The vanilla world is currently in crisis. The cheap prices for vanilla pods/beans following a boom in supply in 2005 has now run its course. Farmers were not encouraged to grow crops, so they burnt their root stocks and chopped down trees to grow other crops, such as palm oil which they felt would afford them a better living. This problem has been hastened by the fact that the demand for artificial vanillin has increased to 95 per cent of the total demand for vanilla flavouring, leaving a market share of only 5 per cent for real vanilla.

Further dangers are emerging from new biotechnologies; for example vanilla and saffron will soon be biotechnologically engineered from yeasts, and will be grown indoors. It is inevitable with the population of Earth growing as it is that other means of feeding the world have to be found. However, this must not be done by stealth. We need to take care of our environments and not turn our back on the flora and fauna of the natural world and the people who depend on it for their living.

It simply cannot be allowed that foodstuffs created in a laboratory, whether from natural root stock or not, can be labelled as a 'natural' product. It's misleading. It is, therefore, very important that we as consumers make ourselves very aware of the source of our foods. The word 'natural' surely relates to something that has been grown and harvested in its natural environment. Correspondingly, 'real' vanilla should only be allowed to be so-called if it is grown in the earth, and comes from a real vanilla orchid vine.

By telling the story of real vanilla and making it affordable, further generations could continue to support the farmers. Patricia Rain, dubbed the 'Vanilla Queen', points out a 1 per cent incursion into the artificial vanilla market would double the need for real vanilla worldwide. Farmers can then start to plan and think ahead knowing that the West will pay for their vanilla. This will then ensure their futures and ours. It is a reciprocal relationship; we buy their vanilla and they look after the ecosystem that is so important to all of us on planet Earth.

The benefits of supporting real vanilla will not only be felt in the equatorial regions. Scientists have not yet isolated all the compounds in vanilla, although they have spent 25 years trying to do so.

There is a scientific investigation currently underway into a special compound in vanilla, that, if isolated, could help to stave off sugar cravings. If these studies were to be proven, imagine how useful this ancient plant could be for the generations to come, to deal with looming obesity problems and the over reliance on sugar in our foods.

We all need to thank the vanilla farmers for their care and labour of vanilla crops. Vanilla belongs to the world but it is those who live alongside it, have tacit knowledge of its behaviour and the expertise in hand pollinating the flowers, that we have to acknowledge and reward. If they choose to abandon vanilla in favour of other more lucrative crops, there is the likelihood of more soil erosion and climatic problems.

Already, weather patterns are showing us year-on-year that something is happening to our fragile earth. We are neglecting our duty to future generations if we do not do our part to help the ecosystem. It may be that in future generations we will all be eating GM foods that have been developed in a lab. That is for the future. However, today and now our ecosystem needs protecting and the people who can do that in the rainforests are the people who live there.

They must be encouraged to cultivate their vanilla crops. With each felling of a tree there are hundreds of habitats lost, gone, never to be recorded. Among them may be the vanilla orchid whose properties may hold the secret which could help future generations.

Who would have thought that baking would be fraught with such important political and ethical decisions?

Making a Difference

Everyone involved in the vanilla industry could be a winner... from the farmer to the consumer and everyone in-between – the cosmetics industry, the pharmaceutical industries and especially the catering industries, whose switch to real vanilla would enrich their products. Nearly all chocolatiers throughout Europe have returned to using real vanilla. Customers can taste the difference and competition is tough. There is immense pride in the industry.

We need this to happen in the kitchens across the world, too. Once consumers connect more with real vanilla they will enjoy not only the improved taste of their food, but they will also be making a valuable contribution to the planet.

You can help in your kitchen. You do not have to go to Madagascar or donate money. You simply have the choice to buy real vanilla. That in itself will encourage the farmers to continue to harvest the crops, safe in the knowledge that demand is constant. Patricia Rain, in particular, has been influential in ameliorating this situation for the farmers, piercing the veil of secrecy that the industry undoubtably suffers from.

The kitchen is where we prepare and eat our daily bread. However the 'daily bread' for the vanilla farmers rests on the choices we make when we purchase our vanilla. By joining the LittlePod Campaign for real vanilla, supporting Blue Ventures' work in Madagascar (http://www.blueventures.org), by joining in with the Vanilla Queen's 1 per cent campaign and mostly by buying real vanilla, the next generation will thank us greatly.

index

acknowledgments

First of all, I would like to thank the contributors to the recipes, particularly Dave Buchanan, LittlePod's development chef, for his fine dining series. For all their help and support the LittlePod team: Clara Milstead, Sam Davey, Tracey Greer, Tom Edwards, Harriet Beesley, George Wheatley, Peter Freeman, Sheila Ogilvie and, of course, Sally Sedgman, our LittlePod ambassador. Also, many thanks to John and Helen Stephens, who helped us get started, Dr Jan Knight for her insights into the science of vanilla, Made Setiawan PhD for his valuable knowledge of growing vanilla and Lloyd Brina for his endless enthusiasm for LittlePod.

Huge thanks also to LP friends: Manju Malhi, the Vanilla Queen, Patricia Rain, Will Halfacree, Ben Thessinger-Wishart in Australia, Richard Heath, Leonel Gouveia and Bertie Cozic. Also, particular thanks go to the Dabell Hotel Group for their hospitality and dedication to customer service and Bickleigh Castle (with special thanks to Sarah Hays) for helping us to launch the very first National Real Vanilla Day.

I would especially like to thank Nathan Joyce, my commissioning editor, for making this book possible. Also, many thanks go to Julia Charles, Leslie Harrington, Lucy McKelvie and the fantastic Steve Painter.

Finally, to my family Dave, Clare and Dan. And for his enduring friendship, Nash.